PRAISE FOR *POWERFU*

MW00450675

Antonetti and Stice turn the bubble-sheet culture (
implementing rigorous and engaging tasks that p
learning. Through Powerful Task Design, *they proviue u wuy of*
goal in the classroom—creating rigorous and engaging tasks that power up learning. I love
this book! The cognitive demand, thinking strategies, and engaging qualities of this book
WILL change the way I interact with my own learners . . . and my two small children.

—**John Almarode, Author**
Visible Learning for Science, Grades K–12 and
From Snorkelers to Scuba Divers
Waynesboro, VA

An easy-to-follow tool for educators wishing to reflect on the rigor of their classroom
tasks with excellent tips to take learning to the next level!

—**Clint Heitz, Instructional Coach**
Bettendorf Community School District, Bettendorf, IA

It is painfully obvious that something needs to be done to do more than simply engage
students; we need to cognitively engage them and this book gives you the tools with
which to do just that. Everything is here for you to make those changes.

—**Melody (Dani) Aldrich, High School English Teacher**
Casa Grande Union High School, Casa Grande, AZ

Finally! A resource that focuses first on the TASK (what it is we are asking of our students)
and then the RESOURCES (what technology is at our disposal to accomplish the task?).
For decades now, the process has been backwards and the focus has become bells-and-
whistle technology that is mistaken for authentic engagement. This book will give tangible
tools for the teacher toolbox while keeping the eye on the rigor prize for students.

—**Matthew Constant, Chief Academic Officer**
Owensboro Public Schools, Owensboro, KY

With this collaboration, Antonetti's expertise with designing engaging and rigorous
student tasks is combined with Stice's vast knowledge of effective technology use in
the classroom. Both Antonetti and Stice have worked with our district's teachers and
administrators and have helped bring about increased teacher effectiveness. This book
is the perfect next step resource for our district's continuous-improvement journey as
well as for any educator ready to effectively take their student-task-design practices to
the next level and meaningfully engage today's 'techie" student.

—**Kelli Bush, Assistant Superintendent for Student Learning**
Elizabethtown Independent Schools, Elizabethtown, KY

As educators, we are on a continuous journey to stretch and grow to our fullest potential
and we all have a "ceiling" of effectiveness. The interactive approach of Powerful Task
Design *will serve as a valuable tool for educators as they stretch and grow toward a*
higher ceiling.

—**Kellianne Wilson, Secondary Instructional Supervisor**
Meade County Schools, KY

Are you grappling with how to create an instructional task that both challenges and engages? Do you continue to struggle with issues related to effective integration of technology into lesson designs? Are you seeking to understand how rigor and engagement can move beyond overused and empty clichés? Explore these and other essential questions in this highly practical, well-researched book that offers practitioner-friendly tools brought to life by a treasure-trove of examples across the content areas of K–12 classrooms. Inviting reflection and personal response at strategic points, the authors skillfully integrate video and other technology with written text to create a book that exhibits the design principles they propose. Powerful Task Design *is a must-read for individual educators and a practical guide for PLCs.*

—**Jackie A. Walsh, Author and Consultant**
Montgomery, AL

Powerful Task Design will help you rethink how to get the full value from the technology tools you have available in your classroom. I found Antonetti and Stice's work to be both practical and transformative. Teachers will come back to this book time and time again as we are challenged to find ways to push thinking, rigor, and engagement to a higher level for our students.

—**Amy Berry, National Board Certified Teacher,**
Coordinator for Student Services
Meade County Schools, KY

Antonetti and Stice push educators to create well-designed tasks that fully engage students and create powerful results. We want the students to learn first and then utilize technology tools to make learning more meaningful. Combining Antonetti's brilliant work with his engagement cube and Stice's technology genius is just "mind-blowing."

—**Allen Martin, Instructional Technology Resource Teacher**
Bowling Green Independent Schools, KY

Antonetti and Stice once again provide outstanding leadership, research, and guidance through an ever-expanding and vital conversation on learning design. This book further shifts the conversation from technology to learning, from simply rehashing techno-centric approaches, to ready-to-implement rich learning experiences for students further empowered through digital tools and resources.

In this book, you'll discover creative solutions to interesting digital instructional design challenges from real classrooms and real students. These best-practice models will help any teacher, new or experienced, formulate a blueprint for digital learning experience design— with a tremendous emphasis on learning and cognitive engagement. I especially love the connections made in Chapter 5 with technology and questions. Through this book, Antonetti and Stice demonstrate that they are two highly connected teachers who "get it."

—**Marty Park, Chief Digital Officer for**
the Office of Education Technology
Kentucky Department of Education, Lexington, KY

Powerful Task Design

Rigorous and Engaging Tasks to Level Up Instruction

John Antonetti

Terri Stice

CORWIN

A SAGE Publishing Company

FOR INFORMATION:

Corwin

A SAGE Company

2455 Teller Road

Thousand Oaks, California 91320

(800) 233-9936

www.corwin.com

SAGE Publications Ltd.

1 Oliver's Yard

55 City Road

London EC1Y 1SP

United Kingdom

SAGE Publications India Pvt. Ltd.

B 1/I 1 Mohan Cooperative Industrial Area

Mathura Road, New Delhi 110 044

India

SAGE Publications Asia-Pacific Pte. Ltd.

3 Church Street

#10-04 Samsung Hub

Singapore 049483

Acquisitions Editor: Ariel Bartlett Curry

Development Editor: Desirée A. Bartlett

Editorial Assistant: Jessica Vidal

Production Editor: Amy Schroller

Copy Editor: Cate Huisman

Typesetter: C&M Digitals (P) Ltd.

Proofreader: Dennis W. Webb

Indexer: Sheila Bodell

Cover Designer: Candice Harman

Marketing Manager: Brian Grimm

Printed in the United States of America

ISBN 978-1-5063-9914-0

This book is printed on acid-free paper.

19 20 21 22 10 9 8 7 6 5 4 3 2

Contents

Acknowledgments   vii

About the Authors   ix

Introduction: The Power of the Task   1

1. The Work of School   7

    A Task Is a Task   9

    Task Predicts Performance   10

    The Design Components of a Task   12

    Technology in a Working Model, or When
       Terri Met Sally (Ahem, John)   13

    The Powerful Task Rubric for Designing Student Work   15

2. Analyzing Learning With the Powerful Task Rubric   27

    One Content, Five Tasks   27

    Where Was the Power?   53

3. The Power of Engagement   57

    The Qualities of Engagement   60

    Interaction as Engagement   64

    A Task Is Powered Up   68

4. The Power of Academic Strategies   75

    It Starts on the Playground   75

    Strategies of Personal Response   76

    Identifying Similarities and Differences   78

    Summarizing and Note-Making   79

    Note-Taking Becomes Note-Making   83

    Reflection in Note-Making   90

    Nonlinguistic Representations   91

    Generating and Testing Hypotheses   95

    Reflection and Closure   107

5. The Power of the Question   109

   Where Does a Question Come From?   109
   See-Think-Wonder   111
   Where Do Teacher Questions Come From?   116
   How to Open a Question   124
   Technology and Questions   131

6. Engaged in *What*? The Power of Cognition   135

   Cognitive Demand   137
   Learning Through Accepting Meaning   140
   Thinking and Making Meaning   141
   Making Meaning on Top of Meaning   144
   Sliding Across the Cognitive Continua:
      A Hierarchy, Not a Sequence   145
   Math Cognition and the Task Rubric   148
   Encoding and Memory   153

7. Power Up: Using the Diagnostic
   Instrument to Analyze Learning   157

   The Diagnostic Instrument to Analyze Learning   158
   Premises and Research Behind the DIAL   158
   Using the DIAL   162
   Three DIAL Implementations   163
   Tips for the Tool   167

8. Putting It All Together   169

Final Thoughts   195

References   197

Index   199

Acknowledgments

Corwin gratefully acknowledges the contributions of the following reviewers:

Melody (Dani) Aldrich, High School English Teacher
Casa Grande Union High School
Casa Grande, AZ

Clint R. Heitz, Instructional Coach
Bettendorf High School
Bettendorf, IA

Michelle Liga, Technology Integration Specialist PreK–Eighth Grade
Kingwood Elementary
Kingwood, WV

Christine Ruder, Second-Grade Teacher
Truman Elementary School
Rolla, MO

Brian Taylor, Director of Science and Engineering Technology K–12
West Islip UFSD
West Islip, NY

About the Authors

John Antonetti is a learner. He has had the great fortune to visit classrooms throughout North America in an effort to answer the question, "What truly engages learners?" From thousands of students in pre-kindergarten through graduate school, John has learned the three facets of powerful learning tasks—intellectual, academic, and emotional engagement.

John Antonetti is a teacher. He has taught AP chemistry and kindergarten and most grades in between in his home state of Arkansas. Once described by Larry Lezotte as a "teacher's teacher," Mr. Antonetti works with schools across the country and Canada on student engagement, writing, rigor and relevance, and high-yield best practices. As the former director of curriculum in the Sheridan School District in Arkansas, he took what he learned in his home district and developed strategies and protocols that work across all school types. He has partnered with five school districts that were awarded the nationally recognized Broad Prize for Urban Education.

While hands-on work in schools is his passion, Antonetti is also a highly sought keynote speaker. His humor and parables are recognized by teachers, administrators, and parents as relevant examples of the power of teachers.

Antonetti is the author of the book *Writing as a Measure and Model of Thinking*, which describes the engagement cube and practical tools to increase student thinking in all subject areas. With his late business partner and friend, Jim Garver, John coauthored the ASCD best-seller *17,000 Classroom Visits Can't Be Wrong: Strategies That Engage Students, Promote Active Learning, and Boost Achievement*.

Whether he's on the carpet with kindergarteners or in front of 4,000 teachers at an international conference, Antonetti continues to learn.

Terri Stice is in her 18th year as the Director of Instructional Technology for the Green River Regional Educational Cooperative, a service agency providing professional learning opportunities for teachers and administrators at the prekindergarten through graduate-school level. Terri custom-designs and facilitates workshops and provides consulting and coaching services in the areas of technology integration, student engagement, literacy/thinking skills, and school culture. Her favorite part of her job is coaching teachers one-on-one in their classrooms. She has been involved with technology to support teaching and learning since the early 1990s, has 15 years of experience as a teacher, and has been a technology coordinator at both the district and school levels.

Ms. Stice holds a master of science degree in instructional media design from Wilkes University in Pennsylvania. She is an Apple Distinguished Educator, an Apple Teacher, an Apple Field Trainer, a Google Certified Teacher, and a Discovery Education Star Educator. She is a recipient of the KYSTE/ISTE Making IT Happen award as well as the 2017 Stilwell Award.

Currently, Terri is also an adjunct professor of educational technology courses at Western Kentucky University.

Terri is committed to lifelong learning and continual growth. Her passion is working with teachers who have the drive and determination to be the best they can be for the learners in their lives.

Introduction
The Power of the Task

Please follow the directions and complete the Iconic Event Task below:

Below is a series of seminal, historical, and influential events that have happened in the United States during the 21st century. If you are American, it is likely that the events have had an impact on your life. Once you have identified/clarified each event below, rank the events from greatest impact in your life to least impact in your life by placing the number for each event on the continuum below the list. Be prepared to justify your rankings. If you need some assistance (or validation) that you are working with the "correct" moments in time, smartphones are excellent tools for acquiring facts quickly. Since acquiring the information is not the goal of this task, but just a precursor to transferring the knowledge of the facts to a new context, we encourage you to use your device or any technology at your disposal.

A digital version of the Iconic Event Task is also available on the companion website at http://resources.corwin.com/powerfultask.

1. A historical election in 2008
2. A series of four coordinated terrorist attacks on the United States
3. An explosive finish in 2013
4. The costliest natural disaster in the history of the United States
5. Mark Zuckerberg changes the meaning of *friend*
6. Everyone survives US Airways flight 1549
7. Death of the "King of Pop"
8. Steve Jobs's announcement in 2007

Least   Greatest

After ranking the events, it's time to make your thinking visible by writing the following:

State your opinion on which is the event of greatest impact.

Support your opinion with the reasons you made the choice you made.

This exercise will become more meaningful and powerful if you share your personal response (opinion and reasoning) with others. If you are reading this text as part of a book study, we would encourage you to have a full discussion about which event had the most impact on you and why. While thoughtfully listening to each individual's point of view, feel free to make notes, capturing others' reactions and thoughts that are both similar to and different from your own response. Once everyone has shared, revisit your original thinking, and decide if you want or need to make any revisions to your work.

If you are reading this book alone, we encourage you to share your thoughts with a family member or colleague. Do they see the events in the same order of impact?

If you are reading alone and do not have access to another opinion, please go to this book's companion website, http://resources.corwin.com/powerfultask, to hear two other thoughts in Video 0.1. You can access the companion website via the QR code below.

Before moving on. . . . Did you actually do the activity? If you chose not to, you may be reading the wrong book. The design of the book is based on the premise that if we do not experience a learning task as a student (or at least from the learner's viewpoint), we cannot truly reflect on its value for the learner. True, we can probably still reflect on the task from an educator's perspective, but this book is about shifting the perspective from the teacher and lesson planning to the learner and task design and implementation.

Seriously, if you did not complete the Iconic Event Task, please return to the instructions and complete the task.

Ok, you're back. Congratulations and thank you. We cannot force you to complete the tasks in the book, but we will assume compliance. (Is compliance in a task necessary for engagement in a task? We'll consider this question later.)

Reflect on Task Design and Value

What did you like about the Iconic Event Task? Why?

What did not like (or like least) in the Iconic Event Task? Why?

What did you find challenging about the Iconic Event Task? Why?

Would the task have been the same if the eight events had been explicitly named? Why? Why not?

If the following standards represent the learning targets of the Iconic Event Task, please consider the task through these two lenses:

D2.His.4.3-5.

Explain why individuals and groups during the same historical period differed in their perspectives.

(Continued)

(Continued)

CCR Writing Anchor Standard #1

1. Write arguments to support claims in an analysis of substantive topics or texts using valid reasoning and relevant and sufficient evidence.

    Do you feel that the task demanded that you perform the social studies standard?

    Why or why not?

    Do you feel that the task demanded that you perform the writing standard?

    Why or why not?

Please consider taking the following task design suggestion back to your classroom.

> **Task to Try**
>
> A continuum can be a powerful tool to organize, expand, and quantify thinking when learners are asked to consider complex concepts. Any time you want to get your students to the evaluation level of thinking, ask them to place concepts on a continuum. The most important part of the task is that students must be able to explain the particular placement of items on the continuum.

The design of the Iconic Event Task captures the inspiration for our work as well as the reason we wanted to write this book: A well-designed task allows learners to make meaning even if the curriculum is based upon a known set of accepted facts, dates, and ideas. While technology is most helpful in retrieving information about the actual eight events (or at least clarifying them), it is the actual design requirement of what to do with this information that provides the powerful learning. Let's take a deeper look at the design of the Iconic Event Task.

The Iconic Event Task is predicated upon the learner clarifying and accurately naming an event, which is a low-level, cognitive-demand task that asks for compliance but no engagement. It simply asks the student to recall information. It has been our experience, in over 20,000 classroom observations, teachers spend lots of time on such tasks. If a student doesn't recall the events, the student is finished and unable to perform the task. Through thoughtful design, our task incorporates the efficient use of technology to allow students to secure the knowledge-level information they need to then move that information into a higher-level task of making meaning. Our learning intention is not to have students name the events; rather it is to have them personalize and process the impact of the events in their personal lives, which requires them to find patterns, compare patterns, and ultimately evaluate and justify their decisions. The Iconic Event Task is a highly engaging and rigorous task made possible by the use of technology.

ABOUT THIS BOOK

We have carefully chosen to chunk the information in this book into manageable pieces, building the Powerful Task Rubric one chapter at a time, pausing frequently to allow the reader opportunities to interact with the text. Also, we have filled this book with a plethora of powerful tasks, representing a variety of content areas as well as grade levels (prekindergarten to high school).

In many cases, we ask you, the reader, to be an active participant and do the tasks. This allows you the chance to experience the learning as your students might. At the same time, you may choose to do a group book study, in which case doing the tasks with colleagues will likely spark ideas and lead to rich discussions about how to improve learning experiences for students. Regardless of how you approach the text, we encourage you to interact with all of the resources and materials included. Do the tasks, watch the videos on the companion website, access and analyze the student work samples, and make use of the tools included throughout the book.

At the end of each chapter, you will find a QR code to the companion website, where you will find all of the videos.

It is our hope you will consider sharing your learning journey with others, including us! You will find us both on twitter at

@JohnAntonetti

@tstice

#PowerfulTaskDesign

http://resources.corwin.com/powerfultask

CHAPTER 1

The Work of School

Kerry, a first grader in southern California, once shared with us his definition of school: "It's a place where you come and they make you do stuff so you'll learn."

We like this definition of school. It is simple, yet profound. Most important, the definition comes from a student perspective, rather than the teacher's perspective. And yet, our first grader recognizes that the basic structure of first grade consists of three parts that we, as teachers, must also distinguish.

"A place where you come and they . . . "	Teachers
". . . make you . . . "	Students
". . . do stuff so you will learn."	Content

While Kerry was figuring out school in California, another group on the East Coast was discovering the same definition. In their seminal work, *Instructional Rounds in Education,* Richard Elmore and his Harvard colleagues state that "there are only three ways to improve student learning at scale."

1. Increase the level of knowledge and skill that the teacher brings to the instructional process.
2. Increase the level and complexity of the content that students are asked to learn.
3. Change the role of the student in the instructional process. (City, Elmore, Fiarman, & Teitel, 2009, p. 24)

Elmore and colleagues argue that to improve instruction we must work on this "Instructional Core" (Figure 1.1), recognizing that we cannot just focus on a single element of the core; all elements must be addressed. That is, one must simultaneously work to improve the teacher's skills and knowledge, the students' level of engagement and participation in learning, and the rigor of the content being taught.

In the center of the Instructional Core is the student task—or in Kerry's words, the stuff they make you *do*. The task is the meeting point of the Instructional Core components. One might call it the end product of the

FIGURE 1.1 Instructional Core

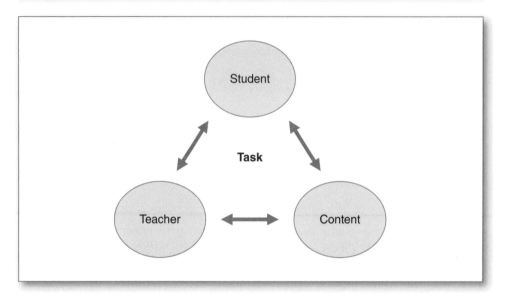

core. Or the entry into the core. For our purposes, it shall be considered the entry point and the design of learning.

Summarizing the work of Walter Doyle, *task* has been defined as "the actual work that students are asked to do in the process of instruction—not what teachers think they are asking students to do, or what the official curriculum says that students are asked to do, but what they are actually asked to do" (City et al., 2009, p. 30).

This book is about the stuff students actually do.

As the authors of the book you are reading, we cannot compel you to do the stuff in the introduction, but we thank you if you completed the activity. The readers who volunteered to complete the task might have chosen to do so because they like following procedures, sequences, rules, and written expectations of school. Perhaps they completed the activity because they want to experience all the book can offer. Other readers may have participated because they found the iconic events interesting or because some of the events were unknown or uncertain. Still other learners may have been drawn into the activity because the end product was open and arguable and allowed personal decisions and answers.

For the readers who chose to skim and skip the activity, we understand (and also thank you for reading the book). You may have desired a faster journey to the actual "content" of this book. You may have a very specific personal focus regarding what you want from this book and need to search for it efficiently.

In either case, we recognize that readers were in complete control of how and why they interacted with the first few pages of this book. The personal

http://resources.corwin.com/powerfultask   POWERFUL TASK DESIGN decisions you made in your participation thus far take us to the essence of the work we are about to explore: Learners are volunteers.

Students will volunteer time and energy (or not) to activities in a classroom for a variety of reasons. Levels of motivation, interest, fear, attraction, sense of duty, and engagement are only some of the factors that result in the wide range of volunteerism or participation in a task.

While the remainder of the book will look at ways to increase volunteerism in scholastic activities and tasks, we must first answer the questions, "What is a task?" and "What is the distinction between activities and tasks?".

A TASK IS A TASK

Let us consider a class in which the teacher wants the learners to be able to "analyze how the author's use of figurative language impacts meaning and tone" of a poem. To that end, each student is independently searching the given poem for examples of figurative language. They are asked to circle the figurative language in the text and annotate whether each occurrence is an example of metaphor, simile, or personification. The task is to find and identify the three types of figurative language or at least recognize the accompanying triggers or clues (e.g., the word *like* in a simile). This does not mean that students can now "analyze how the author's use of figurative language impacts meaning and tone." That is a different task with a particular cognitive demand, and the students did not do that work.

In order to provide a more precise language for the rest of this book, we want to drill down further and provide additional clarification about the difference between a task and an activity. For us, a task always includes a cognitive expectation or cognitive demand. An activity involves the other pieces that surround or support the cognitive task. In our poetry example, students obviously must be able to decode and comprehend the actual words they are reading, but this is not the purpose or goal of the planned task of finding and identifying figurative language. (We have watched students who were successful in identifying simile because the word *like* was present in the text, while not comprehending the words in the simile or the meaning of the comparison.)

Sometimes the work is practice and repetition of a skill set with a goal of increased accuracy and speed. At other times, the

> A task always includes a cognitive expectation or cognitive demand.

task is one of inquiry, wherein students are asked to make sense of and find patterns in the content. Both of these are tasks, because they have a cognitive demand.

The relationship between activity and task is quite interesting. There is almost always interdependence between the two. If you can't read the problem (activity), you can't solve it using the Pythagorean theorem. An overwhelming activity—one that is "bigger" or more engaging than the cognition desired—can also diminish or even erase the intent of the task.

In a fourth-grade social studies class, the students have spent the first of three class sessions looking at background material before completing a Document Based Question (DBQ) protocol to determine "What caused the Dust Bowl?" Before they dig deeper into primary and secondary sources to research the question, the teacher presents the next task: "Now that we have some background information, I want you to get into groups of four and make three predictions about possible answers to the question. You will have ten minutes and then we will share with the class your ideas. Be prepared to explain your group's ideas." (Note: If you are familiar with the DBQ Project, this is the "pre-bucketing" task.)

Let's now watch a group of students interact with the task.

As our group comes together, Sharon jumps right in. "I think the dust bowl was caused when they killed the shortgrass prairie and all the dirt got blown into the air." Immediately, Anne counters with, "I think there were too many people farming." Livi-Kate adds, "The depression made people leave their farms and that caused the dust bowl." All the while, Brianna is listening to her table mates, verbally agreeing with their ideas and cheering them on. She fills in her bucket graphic organizer successfully, yet she has not completed the cognitive task. In this case, the collaborative structure of the activity allowed Brianna to opt out of the task.

As you are reading this scenario, you may be thinking that there is an easy fix to this situation. Each of the girls in the group could be required to first work independently in proposing one or two predictions and committing those ideas in writing on a sticky note before she works with the group. The activity would now guarantee that the task is required of each learner and will most likely produce more ideas and better conversations as the girls work to compare or combine their ideas. In this case, the "entrance ticket" into the collaborative activity may be more important to the task guarantee than the "exit ticket."

> All tasks are activities, but not all activities are tasks.

The simple change the teacher makes to the original activity/task transforms the experience the learners have with the content, especially for Brianna.

TASK PREDICTS PERFORMANCE

Richard Elmore's phrase "the task predicts performance" has been quoted numerous times by many and with good reason. The examples we've used above are perfect illustrations of this point: The students in our poetry class are not likely able to analyze the relationship between figurative language and tone, simply because they did not accomplish that task. If Brianna participated in the dust bowl activity only as the recorder of ideas, we should not assume that Brianna can do this work independently.

At any given moment in a school, the activity within a classroom might be to listen, or watch, or participate in a discussion. Certainly, learning can occur by listening and watching, but we cannot ascertain learning until the student has the "forced opportunity" to mimic, repeat, react, analyze, or respond to that which she has heard or seen. In other words, until there is an articulated task completed by each individual student, there is no guarantee of thinking or learning.

> Until there is an articulated task completed by each individual student, there is no guarantee of thinking or learning.

In 2005, John partnered with Dr. James R. Garver to formalize the work he had begun in 2001—defining engagement through the lens of the learner. Using the Look 2 Learning classroom walk-through protocol they developed and continued to refine, Antonetti and Garver visited 17,124 classrooms in the United States and Canada. The protocol is based on a short interview with students involved in learning activities to analyze the engagement value and impact of the core task. Antonetti and Garver quickly learned that to look for student engagement, they would have to almost ignore two of the components in the instructional core—teachers and content—and focus first on the students and their interaction with and within the task at hand.

Teachers who walked with Antonetti and Garver were often surprised (and sometimes horrified) at their purposeful disregard of the teacher. While the teacher is always part and parcel of the learning, Antonetti and Garver assure teachers that the truest picture of learning comes from focusing first on the students and the work they are doing in the classroom. Certainly, the role of the teacher and the content shifts and morphs with the design of the task. For example, if students are learning a mathematical procedure or how to conjugate regular -ir verbs in French class, they may be asked to repeat the procedure for the first time (one task) and then practice a procedure through four or five additional examples. In each case, the task demands a specific role for the teacher—the first begins with modeling and demonstrating and then shifts to monitoring and providing feedback. The content may become more complex as the students experience success, or the content may be backed down as the teacher decides to break the procedure into smaller chunks.

To accurately capture and isolate the myriad cognitive, social, and communal layers represented in a single 20-minute lesson is almost impossible. Antonetti and Garver focused on only the task and then asked teachers to personally and collaboratively reflect on the relationship between the task data and their students, the task data and teacher practice, and the task data and the content.

One of the most interesting data sets regarding the relationship between activity and task captures what percentage of class time students are involved in listening or watching (Figure 1.2). To be clear, the percentages in the chart represent the amount of time students were involved in activities of listening and watching that did not have an articulated task. For example, students might be asked to listen and watch as the teacher explained imperialism in Africa in the 1900s. They might also be asked to record notes as they listened. For some, the act of note-taking might involve a higher cognitive task of the student's own design, but for the majority of students, the activity produced "writing" that guaranteed only simple repetition of the words or thoughts presented in the lecture—regardless of student understanding.

FIGURE 1.2 Primary Student Activity by Grade Cluster

Grade Levels	Activities Involving Listening/Watching
All Classrooms (PreK–Grade 12)	49%
Primary (PreK–Grade 2)	37%
Intermediate (Grades 3–5)	43%
Middle School (Grades 6–8)	52%
High School (Grades 9–12)	63%

Look 2 Learning Sample size: 17,124 classroom visits

Source: Antonetti & Garver (2015, p. 116).

As you can see in this data, the frequency of listening/watching activities changes as we move through the grade levels. Yet, a significant amount of time is spent in all grades where the passive activity of receiving information may cover up or even replace a more powerful cognitive task. To reconnect to Elmore's instructional core, this data can now be shared with teachers, academic coaches, and school administrators, as they propose relationships between the task and the student, the task and the teacher, and the content targets and the task.

THE DESIGN COMPONENTS OF A TASK

After watching and comparing thousands of student activities, Antonetti and Garver defined three components of a learning task:

Cognitive Demand—the minimal thinking a task will require of the learners

Thinking Strategies—the required visible evidence of Personal Response

Engaging Qualities—the elements and conditions that elicit energy and enthusiasm

In the book, *17,000 Classroom Visits Can't Be Wrong: Strategies That Engage Students, Promote Active Learning, and Boost Achievement* (ASCD, 2015), Antonetti and Garver present these design components, building one upon the other, to ultimately produce a tool for teachers to use when analyzing, developing, or refining tasks to be more cognitively engaging. This book will begin where that volume ended.

TECHNOLOGY IN A WORKING MODEL, OR WHEN TERRI MET SALLY (AHEM, JOHN)

In 2009, John was contracted by Liz Storey, executive director of Green River Regional Educational Cooperative (GRREC) in Kentucky, to deliver a keynote address at a school leadership conference in Lexington, Kentucky. Liz introduced John to Terri as the go-to person for any technical support he might need for his presentation. She added that Terri was a master at the integration of technology for learning.

During his presentation, Terri was introduced to John's original Engagement Cube (Figure 1.3). John used the Engagement Cube to show the relationships among the three design components of the tasks he had witnessed bring out the most energy, reasoning, and creativity in learners across the continent. Terri immediately recognized the engaging qualities on the front of the cube as the reasons technology was so powerful for student learning. In an initial conversation between the two, John agreed with Terri, but mentioned that his research was not finding powerful integration of technology in the field.

If you ever played with a Rubik's Cube, you understand the meaning behind the Engagement Cube. As we struggle to solve the puzzle, many of us concentrate our cognitive energy on one facet at a time. We might "fix" the red side only to discover that the other five sides remained a mess. We would then put our energy into "orange," but "blue" would suffer. When we finally solved for yellow, we had again lost red. Sadly, we can find this exercise in our profession—the endless movement of staff development. If you have taught for longer than five years, you may be familiar with this issue. We may concentrate our energy on Initiative A for two years and then switch over to Focus B as required by new standards, a change in leadership, or simply following the next bandwagon.

What the cube really taught us was that there is no single entity that increases engagement. There is no silver bullet! Rather, cognitive engagement is the product of three different variables that come together to solve the puzzle of powerful learning.

As we work with teachers and schools in North America, we use the Engagement Cube as a visual model—a reminder to design learning with all three of the components activated.

FIGURE 1.3 The Cube

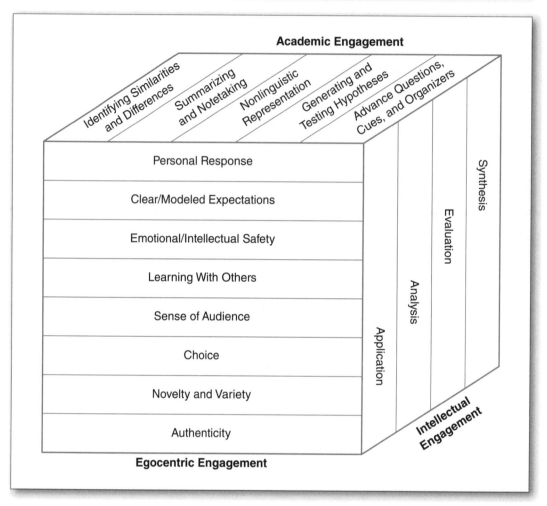

Source: Antonetti (2008).

The original version of the Engagement Cube was first developed by John and teachers in his home school district in Arkansas. In the early 1990s, the state switched its testing model to a more rigorous assessment in math and language arts that required students to work at cognitive levels of application or higher on as much as 40%–60% of the exams. In response to dismal results the first year, John and his faculty decided they needed some help in increasing the student thinking in their daily lessons. His leadership team developed the Engagement Cube as a model to consider during the planning process. Grade-level teams would meet in their professional learning communities (PLCs) to plan engaging, thoughtful lessons with the cube in front of them. As they considered any given standard or objective, the cube provided three questions: What will we have the students do so that they use the higher-level thinking (from the side)? What strategy (from the top) will be required in their writing or explanation? What engaging qualities (from the front) will make them want to do it?

The collaboratively designed experiment was implemented in the class-rooms, and teachers would reflect on the lesson and analyze student work the following week. This cycle of collaboration brought about great improvement in the state test scores, and soon teachers and administrators from across Arkansas were visiting the school to see our planning cycle.

The three-dimensional model made sense to most visitors, but the "how-to" seemed to be lacking—because every teacher defined each of the "line items" in the cube differently.

John came to the realization that rather than fight the many definitions peo-ple brought to the items in the cube, he should capitalize on the progression of ideas that teachers articulated. For example, the engaging quality of Personal Response is present in the question, "What is your favorite color?" But the quality progresses in sophistication of thought when we ask the question, "What color do you think best represents your personality? Why?"

When he began to put each quality or strategy on a progression, or a contin-uum, the Engagement Cube took on the look of a rubric (Figure 1.4). Over the course of 12 years, Antonetti continued to refine the rubric until it took on the form published in *17,000 Classroom Visits Can't Be Wrong: Strategies That Engage Students, Promote Active Learning, and Boost Achievement* (Antonetti and Garver, 2015).

Following the release of *17,000 Classroom Visits*, John was often asked about technology. One workshop participant asked straight out, "How do you write a book about student learning in 2015 without including a chapter on tech-nology?" John paused and then answered, " We did not include a chapter on technology. Nor did we include chapters on desks, pencils, air conditioning, or libraries. We assume schools have all of these things and they can certainly support the learning, but they are not design elements of powerful tasks."

In the subsequent years that John and Terri have worked together and vis-ited an additional 3,500 classrooms, we both have witnessed—and one of us has come to recognize what the other already knew—that technology deserves its own distinction as a design component to bring about more profound learning. As John and Terri continued to work with classroom teachers and administrators, the rubric took on a different look, and a more practical tool emerged (Figure 1.5).

THE POWERFUL TASK RUBRIC FOR DESIGNING STUDENT WORK

If you have ever watched a television infomercial, you know how they sell the product. As quickly as possible, the audience is given a chance to see how to use the product, and to experience it visually. That's what we would like to do at this time: show the tool, and let you play with it. We can spend the rest of the book explaining the components and using the tool to analyze, design, and refine tasks of learning.

FIGURE 1.4 The Original Powerful Task Rubric

The "Rigor Divide" ⟶

	Power Component	1	2	3	4
Cognitive Demand	Bloom – Revised Taxonomy	Recall	Understand	Apply/Analyze	Evaluate/Create
	Examples	Name the steps	Follow the steps	Infer with text support	Argue, defend, or justify
	Antonetti/Garver – Patterns	Repeat patterns	Restate or reproduce patterns	Find patterns Find use for patterns	Compare patterns Add/combine/ignore patterns
	Webb – DOK (Assessment)	Recall	Skill/Concept	Strategic thinking	Extended thinking
	Stein/Smith – Mathematics	Memorization	Procedures without connections	Procedures with connections	Doing Mathematics
Academic Strategies*	Similarities and Differences	List facts about A and B	Parallel facts about A and B	Compare or contrast by trait	
	Summarizing/Notetaking	Copy	Restate	Personalize or make unique decisions about content	
	Nonlinguistic Representation	Copy other given forms	Place into other forms	Create a new representation	
	Generating/Testing Hypotheses	Copy	Restate "known" pattern	Identify and extend patterns	

Power Component	1	2	3	4
Engaging Qualities**				
Personal Response (Clear/Modeled Expectations)	Not necessary	Fill in the blank with "my" answer	Explain and support my ideas (open)	Explain and defend or justify my ideas
Intellectual/Emotional Safety	Not required	Not required	Expression of concepts or recognized patterns	Expression of supported opinions or new ideas
Learning With Others	Take turns talking	Listen and repeat	Interdependence in roles or mini tasks	Interdependence of ideas
Sense of Audience	A partner	The class	An audience I want to appreciate me or my ideas	An audience I want to influence
Novelty and Variety	Recall is fun or different	Product without concepts	Product with concepts	Perspective
Authenticity	Teacher connects to world	Repeat real examples	Recognize real examples	Create real examples
Questions	Closed with single right or wrong answers	Closed but with a "choice" of answers	Open with a range of answers, support, strategies, connections	

17

FIGURE 1.5 The Powerful Task Rubric

The "Rigor Divide"

	Power Component	1	2	3	4
Cognitive Demand	Bloom – Revised Taxonomy *Examples*	Recall Name the steps	Understand Follow the steps	Apply/Analyze Infer with text support	Evaluate/Create Argue, defend, or justify
	Antonetti/Garver/Stice – Meaning	Repeat accepted meaning	Restate or reproduce accepted meaning	Making meaning: Find patterns Find use for patterns	Compare patterns Add/combine/ignore patterns
	Webb – DOK (Assessment)	Recall	Skill/Concept	Strategic thinking	Extended thinking
	Stein/Smith – Mathematics	Memorization	Procedures without connections	Procedures with connections	Making sense
Connected Learning (Tech)	Antonetti/Stice	Retrieve Copy & paste	Click here, click here, click . . . Prescriptive Learning Accessible Learning	Control- Interests power learning Question, share, contribute, Link, provide feedback	Produce, create Experiment, Design
Academic Strategies*	Similarities and Differences	List facts about A and B	Parallel facts about A and B	Compare or contrast by trait	
	Summarizing/Note-making	Copy	Restate	Personalize or make unique decisions about content	
	Nonlinguistic Representation	Copy other given forms	Place into other forms	Create a new representation	
	Generating/Testing Hypotheses	Copy	Restate "known" pattern	Identify and extend patterns	

	Power Component	1	2	3	4
Engaging Qualities**	Personal Response (Clear/Modeled Expectations)	Not necessary	Fill in the blank with "my" answer	Explain and support my ideas (open)	Explain and defend or justify my ideas
	Intellectual/Emotional Safety	Not required	Not required	Expression of concepts or recognized patterns	Expression of supported opinions or new ideas
	Learning With Others	Take turns talking	Listen and repeat	Interdependence in roles or mini tasks	Interdependence of ideas
	Sense of Audience	A partner	The class	An audience I want to appreciate me or my ideas	An audience I want to influence
	Novelty and Variety	Recall is fun or different	Product without concepts	Product with concepts	Perspective
	Authenticity	Teacher connects to world	Repeat real examples	Recognize real examples	Create real examples
	Questions	Closed with single right or wrong answers	Closed but with a "choice" of answers	Open with a range of answers, support, strategies, connections	

*The strategies listed are those directly influencing rigor or cognitive demand.

**The engaging quality of choice is not listed; it is effectively provided through choice between rigorous tasks.

online resources

19

As you can see in the left column, the Task Rubric consists of the three components of cognition, strategy, and engaging qualities. Technology and questioning are additional design components that impact learning. Rather than being a tool that evaluates a task as good or bad, strong or weak, the Task Rubric presents a series of continua that recognize the fluidity of design elements. This will allow the user to objectively "find" the value of a task, rather than make evaluative judgments about a task. In other words, we do not want the user to see things on the left side of a continuum to be weak or to see things on the right as optimal. The evaluation of a task depends on its intended purpose.

For example, if our students need to practice multiplication facts for speed and accuracy, a task that falls at Level 1 (the column from the rubric) would be serving its intended purpose: recall, memorization (Figure 1.6).

FIGURE 1.6 Tasks at Level 1 of Cognitive Demand

	Power Component	*1*	*2*	*3*	*4*
Cognitive Demand	Bloom – Revised Taxonomy	Recall (circled)	Understand	Apply/Analyze	Evaluate/Create
	Examples	Name the steps	Follow the steps	Infer with text support	Argue, defend, or justify
	Antonetti/Garver – Patterns	Repeat patterns	Restate or reproduce patterns	Find patterns Find use for patterns	Compare patterns Add/combine/ ignore patterns
	Webb – DOK (Assessment)	Recall	Skill/Concept	Strategic thinking	Extended thinking
	Stein/Smith – Mathematics	Memorization (circled)	Procedures without connections	Procedures with connections	Making sense

Later in that same classroom, students are given a mathematical scenario that is new to them, and they struggle to find an entry point into a mathematical situation. Now the cognitive demand is at a Level 3 or 4 (Figure 1.7). (Note: We will not worry about accuracy at this time in our exploration of the tool. Rather, we want to develop some comfort in the idea of placing tasks against the continua.)

In addition to analyzing where a task falls on the continua, we can also look at the relationships among design elements. To illustrate, let's consider the role of the engaging quality of Personal Response found in the fourth row from the top in the rubric. In our first math task of memorizing

FIGURE 1.7 Tasks at Levels 3 and 4 of Cognitive Demand

	Power Component	1	2	3	4
Cognitive Demand	Bloom – Revised Taxonomy	Recall	Understand	Apply/Analyze	Evaluate/Create
	Examples	Name the steps	Follow the steps	Infer with text support	Argue, defend, or justify
	Antonetti/Garver – Patterns	Repeat patterns	Restate or reproduce patterns	Find patterns Find use for patterns	Compare patterns Add/combine/ ignore patterns
	Webb – DOK (Assessment)	Recall	Skill/Concept	Strategic thinking	Extended thinking
	Stein/Smith – Mathematics	Memorization	Procedures without connections	Procedures with connections	Making sense

FIGURE 1.8 Level 1 Personal Response

Personal Response (Clear/Modeled Expectations)	Not necessary	Fill in the blank with "my" answer	Explain and support my ideas (open)	Explain and defend or justify my ideas

multiplication facts, Personal Response is neither necessary nor even desired. In other words, the answer to 4 × 4 should be 16, no matter who you are or what your background experiences have been. An answer of 17 is not Personal Response; it's just incorrect (Figure 1.8).

In our second task, the nature of the mathematics allows for students to find different ways into the math and to use different strategies and protocols. The task moves further along the continuum of engagement as students explain and support their ideas.

While we will eventually unpack each component and the associated continua in the rubric, we feel it is important to start with the end in mind and jump into a full task analysis. That said, let us return to the Iconic Event Task and compare the learning experience to the Task Rubric.

Use the Powerful Task Rubric in Figure 1.9 or follow the QR code at the end of this chapter to retrieve a copy from the companion website to capture

FIGURE 1.9 Rubric for Analysis of Iconic Events Task

⇨ The "Rigor Divide"

	Power Component	1	2	3	4
Cognitive Demand	Bloom – Revised Taxonomy *Examples*	Recall Name the steps	Understand Follow the steps	Apply/Analyze Infer with text support	Evaluate/Create Argue, defend, or justify
	Antonetti/Garver/Stice – Meaning	Repeat accepted meaning	Restate or reproduce accepted meaning	Making meaning: Find patterns Find use for patterns	Compare patterns Add/combine/ignore patterns
	Webb – DOK (Assessment)	Recall	Skill/Concept	Strategic thinking	Extended thinking
	Stein/Smith – Mathematics	Memorization	Procedures without connections	Procedures with connections	Making sense
Connected Learning (Tech)	Antonetti/Stice	Retrieve Copy & paste	Click here, click here, click . . . Prescriptive Learning Accessible Learning	Control- Interests power learning Question, share, contribute, Link, provide feedback	Produce, create Experiment, Design
Academic Strategies*	Similarities and Differences	List facts about A and B	Parallel facts about A and B	Compare or contrast by trait	
	Summarizing/Note-making	Copy	Restate	Personalize or make unique decisions about content	
	Nonlinguistic Representation	Copy other given forms	Place into other forms	Create a new representation	
	Generating/Testing Hypotheses	Copy	Restate "known" pattern	Identify and extend patterns	

Power Component	1	2	3	4
Personal Response (Clear/Modeled Expectations)	Not necessary	Fill in the blank with "my" answer	Explain and support my ideas (open)	Explain and defend or justify my ideas
Intellectual/Emotional Safety	Not required	Not required	Expression of concepts or recognized patterns	Expression of supported opinions or new ideas
Learning With Others	Take turns talking	Listen and repeat	Interdependence in roles or mini tasks	Interdependence of ideas
Sense of Audience	A partner	The class	An audience I want to appreciate me or my ideas	An audience I want to influence
Novelty and Variety	Recall is fun or different	Product without concepts	Product with concepts	Perspective
Authenticity	Teacher connects to world	Repeat real examples	Recognize real examples	Create real examples
Questions	Closed with single right or wrong answers	Closed but with a "choice" of answers	Open with a range of answers, support, strategies, connections	

*Engaging Qualities***

*The strategies listed are those directly influencing rigor or cognitive demand.

**The engaging quality of choice is not listed; it is effectively provided through choice between rigorous tasks.

online resources

your interaction with the Iconic Events Task in the Introduction. Be sure to mark all indicators that are accurate descriptions of your experience.

After completing your first analysis using the Powerful Task Rubric (Figure 1.5), please answer the following questions:

What is your initial reaction to the rubric?

What components (phrases, or relationships) make the most sense at this time?

What components (phrases, or relationships) are confusing at this time?

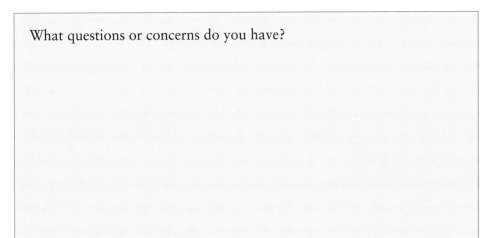

What questions or concerns do you have?

According to John Hattie (2012), visible learning and teaching occurs when teachers see learning through the eyes of students and then use this experience to become better teachers. The Powerful Task Rubric for Designing Student Work is a tool that allows both the design of the task and the actual implementation of the task to become visible to teachers, professional learning communities, and administrators.

When we remove the teacher and the content, we can look at the task through the student's eyes. For this reason, the Task Rubric can be used across all disciplines and grade levels. Let's dig into some social studies in Chapter 2!

http://resources.corwin.com/powerfultask

CHAPTER 2

Analyzing Learning With the Powerful Task Rubric

As educators, we would like to post our objective/focus for this chapter before we jump into it. The awkward truth is that we don't have a single focus for these pages; rather, we have two separate objectives to put forth.

Objective #1: To experience as learners the progression of a series of content tasks as cognition deepens and engagement and strategy increase.

Objective #2: To analyze the relationships between (and interdependence of) the three design components to increase the rigor of a task.

ONE CONTENT, FIVE TASKS

Over the next few pages, we ask the reader to complete a sequence of five social studies tasks. The tasks may build one upon another, but we will stop after each and ask you to reflect as a learner (Objective #1) and then place each task on the Task Rubric for analysis (Objective #2).

Note to reader: Since most of the tasks have the engaging quality of Learning With Others as part of the task design, we will provide examples of small groups performing certain tasks on our companion website, which you can access through QR codes at the end of each chapter or by going to http://resources.corwin.com/powerfultask. Since our analysis of each task design will be based upon the learners in the videos, we encourage you to watch the clips, especially if you are alone while reading this book.

Each content activity will be presented as a question to answer as well as a task to perform.[1]

---

[1]A note of apology to our international readers: The content may be US history, but you will not be at a disadvantage.

Question #1

What are the five rights (or freedoms) guaranteed in the First Amendment to the US Constitution?

Task #1

In the space below, list the five rights (or freedoms) guaranteed in the First Amendment to the US Constitution. Please make sure your answers are correct and accurate. You may phone a friend. You may use technology. Do not guess.

My answer: 1.

2.

3.

4.

5.

Task #1 has a single set of correct answers. For that reason, let us first consider the cognitive demand of the task (Figure 2.1). Using any continuum indicators provided in this row of the rubric, find and mark the best description of the thinking in this task: Level 1, 2, 3, or 4.

Before we move forward, please follow the QR code at the end of this chapter to our companion website to watch how two other groups of learners completed the task.

FIGURE 2.1 Cognitive Demand of Task #1

	Power Component	1	2	3	4
Cognitive Demand	Bloom – Revised Taxonomy *Examples*	Recall Name the steps	Understand Follow the steps	Apply/Analyze Infer with text support	Evaluate/Create Argue, defend, or justify
	Antonetti/Garver/ Stice – Meaning	Repeat accepted meaning	Restate or reproduce accepted meaning	Making meaning: Find patterns Find use for patterns	Compare patterns Add/combine/ ignore patterns
	Webb – DOK (Assessment)	Recall	Skill/Concept	Strategic thinking	Extended thinking
	Stein/Smith – Mathematics	Memorization	Procedures without connections	Procedures with connections	Making sense

While the obvious placement of this task might be a Level 1 *recall*, the videos show a different story. In the first segment (Video 2.1), the learners are successful in the task because Emma Grace (in the white shirt) was confident in her recall of the five rights. Because Emma Grace was the source of the correct answers, we would say that the other members of the group did not have to bear the cognitive demand. In other words, Emma Grace worked at a cognition of Level 1, while the others were successful simply because they had her in the group. The collaborative design of the task diminished the guaranteed cognitive load for *each* individual learner to zero.

In the second video segment (Video 2.2), the learners chose to use technology, as was suggested in the instructions. While we can celebrate the learners' ability to find the answers on their devices, the use of technology in what could have been a Level 1 demand actually removed the human cognition. Another way to say this is Siri gets credit for a Level 1 demand while our living learners get credit for writing down what Siri said. Remember that the rubric is not a measure of the learner, so the learner is not judged for choosing to use technology to get the correct answers. As we analyze the task—not the learner—the role of technology is marked on the rubric as shown in Figure 2.2.

FIGURE 2.2 Role of Technology Shown on the Rubric

Connected Learning (Tech)	Antonetti/Stice	Retrieve Copy & paste	Click here, click here, click . . . Prescriptive Learning Accessible Learning	Control- Interests power learning Question, share, contribute, Link, provide feedback	Produce, create Experiment, Design

This moment provides one of the biggest trends we see in classrooms—one we may wish to fight. When technology is added to a Level 1 or Level 2 task, the power of the device may completely erase the cognition for the learner. This is especially troublesome if the endpoint of the lesson plan was to *Recall* or *Understand*. We have actually seen students enter the phrase "five freedoms guaranteed in first amendment" in a search engine that takes them to a blog that presents the five rights—including the right to self-medicate! As you know, this is not a guarantee in the First Amendment, but students who record what they found on the Internet just got the question wrong.

Sometimes technophobes like to quote (misquote?) us on this point. "See, technology reduces thinking. I knew we should not let the kids use their devices."

> If the end goal of the lesson plan is to use the information or apply it to a new situation, using technology to retrieve information allows all learners to begin their cognition from the same starting place.

If the end goal of the lesson plan is to use the information or apply it to a new situation, using technology to retrieve information (that starts at a Level 0) allows all learners to begin their cognition from the same starting place. Technology can provide an important foundation for English language learners, students of poverty, and children who have not had the advantage of previous content instruction to quickly and efficiently access this information so that they may use it to make meaning at a higher level.

We now can continue to place this task on the rubric as we consider the strategies the learners used to make meaning as well as the engaging qualities of Task #1. But since the cognitive demand of the task was a zero, we won't bother. In other words, we don't care what strategies the students used when they "weren't" thinking. Likewise, we will not ask how engaged you were when you weren't being cognitive.

The task demand (guaranteed for all) is a zero. Period. That does not mean it is a bad task. We could even say that this was simply an activity (rather than the learning task), since it simply provides information we now can move further across the rubric. So let's move.

Question #2

What are the five rights (or freedoms) guaranteed in the First Amendment to the US Constitution?

Task #2

Select one of the five rights guaranteed in the First Amendment to the US Constitution and draw a picture of that right in the space provided below. Do not label your picture or share with your friends which right you are drawing.

If you are completing this task privately, please watch the video on the companion website, Video 2.3, to see a group in action.

Since *this* task is more than a "cognitive zero," we invite you to mark the Task Rubric in Figure 2.3 to inspect and capture the task value.

Before we share our thoughts on the value of Task #2, we would like to introduce an important idea to task design and analysis of task: rigor.

With admirable intentions, state agencies, professional organizations, and school districts all ask teachers to increase the rigor in their classrooms. Sadly this request often comes without training or even clear definitions of what rigor is. Like the word *engagement, rigor* has been thrown about education for quite some time—and has therefore become a word with many definitions and misconceptions. We would like to clean that up right now.

Rigor in a task is not a single entity. It is not difficulty. It is not complexity. Rather, it is the product of our three intentional design components: cognition, strategy, and engaging qualities. If one of the components is missing, we may hear our students share the following perspectives:

- Without engaging qualities built in the design, "I don't want to do this. It's too hard."
- Without cognitive engagement, "I'll just accept what I'm told to think."
- Without academic strategies, "I don't know how to think."

Thus, rigor occurs when learners formulate their own unique thoughts of content and strategy and are engaged enough to persevere.

FIGURE 2.3 Task Rubric for Analysis of Task #2

The "Rigor Divide"

	Power Component	1	2	3	4
Cognitive Demand	Bloom – Revised Taxonomy *Examples*	Recall Name the steps	Understand Follow the steps	Apply/Analyze Infer with text support	Evaluate/Create Argue, defend, or justify
	Antonetti/Garver/Stice – Meaning	Repeat accepted meaning	Restate or reproduce accepted meaning	Making meaning: Find patterns Find use for patterns	Compare patterns Add/combine/ignore patterns
	Webb – DOK (Assessment)	Recall	Skill/Concept	Strategic thinking	Extended thinking
	Stein/Smith – Mathematics	Memorization	Procedures without connections	Procedures with connections	Making sense
Connected Learning (Tech)	Antonetti/Stice	Retrieve Copy & paste	Click here, click here, click … Prescriptive Learning Accessible Learning	Control- Interests power learning Question, share, contribute, Link, provide feedback	Produce, create Experiment, Design
Academic Strategies*	Similarities and Differences	List facts about A and B	Parallel facts about A and B	Compare or contrast by trait	
	Summarizing/Note-making	Copy	Restate	Personalize or make unique decisions about content	
	Nonlinguistic Representation	Copy other given forms	Place into other forms	Create a new representation	
	Generating/Testing Hypotheses	Copy	Restate "known" pattern	Identify and extend patterns	

Power Component	1	2	3	4
Personal Response (Clear/Modeled Expectations)	Not necessary	Fill in the blank with "my" answer	Explain and support my ideas (open)	Explain and defend or justify my ideas
Intellectual/Emotional Safety	Not required	Not required	Expression of concepts or recognized patterns	Expression of supported opinions or new ideas
Learning With Others	Take turns talking	Listen and repeat	Interdependence in roles or mini tasks	Interdependence of ideas
Sense of Audience	A partner	The class	An audience I want to appreciate me or my ideas	An audience I want to influence
Novelty and Variety	Recall is fun or different	Product without concepts	Product with concepts	Perspective
Authenticity	Teacher connects to world	Repeat real examples	Recognize real examples	Create real examples
Questions	Closed with single right or wrong answers	Closed but with a "choice" of answers	Open with a range of answers, support, strategies, connections	

*Engaging Qualities***

*The strategies listed are those directly influencing rigor or cognitive demand.

**The engaging quality of choice is not listed; it is effectively provided through choice between rigorous tasks.

online resources

> Rigor occurs when learners formulate their own unique thoughts of content and strategy and are engaged enough to persevere.

With this definition in mind, the Powerful Task Rubric (Figure 1.5) has a double-wide line between Levels 2 and 3 that we call the *rigor divide*. When all three components cross the rigor divide, we deem the task to be rigorous. Another important qualifier to rigor is that it only occurs when the learners have unique, original, or new thoughts. In other words, acceptance of a previously stated idea cannot be a rigorous task. That means there is no such thing as rigorous teaching, only rigorous tasks—designed and facilitated by a teacher. (Teachers can certainly learn in their own professional development—especially if the training involves rigorous tasks rather than somebody reading from PowerPoint slides!)

In our Task #2, did you have an original thought as you drew your picture, *or* did you draw a picture of freedom of religion, or speech, or press, or petition, or assembly? If it is one of the latter, we would contend that those are not *your* ideas; they are presented in the actual First Amendment. So as we each completed the task, we *accepted* the idea(s) presented in the US Constitution. Therefore, the task cannot be considered rigorous.

This is an important—yet difficult to accept—qualifier to rigor. Most adults want to say that Task #2 caused them to do analysis and strategic thinking, that the picture was an explanation of their unique thought. This may be true for some, but most participants admit that they chose to draw the right that was "easiest to draw" or the "one I knew best."

Sometimes in our workshops, teachers will want to push back on us at this point. "This was a good task. I thought it had rigor!" Our response: It *is* a good task. It has great value to the learner. *And* it is not rigorous.

Figure 2.4 shows where we place this task on the rubric.[2]

Again, we place the cognitive demand at a Level 2. The picture is yours, but it is typically a restatement of understanding—you knew what the right was and you already knew what it "looked" like. If your cognition went beyond a 2, congratulations! Other students could have been equally successful in the task by working "only" at a Level 2. Cognitive demand is the minimal expectation of thinking required for successful completion of a task.

What made the task feel personalized and more thoughtful comes from the required strategy you used as you re-*presented* one of the rights. (The name of the strategy even incorporates the word *representation*.) The Nonlinguistic Representation combined with the Personal Response of "my version" of the right occurs at a Level 2.

---

[2]Since there is no technology in this task, we have included a condensed version of the rubric.

FIGURE 2.4 Task #2 Analysis

	Power Component	1	2	3	4
Cognitive Demand	Bloom – Revised Taxonomy *Examples*	Recall Name the steps	Understand Follow the steps	Apply/Analyze Infer with text support	Evaluate/Create Argue, defend, or justify
	Antonetti/Garver/Stice – Meaning	Repeat accepted meaning	Restate or reproduce accepted meaning	Making meaning: Find patterns Find use for patterns	Compare patterns Add/combine/ignore patterns
	Webb – DOK (Assessment)	Recall	Skill/Concept	Strategic thinking	Extended thinking
	Stein/Smith – Mathematics	Memorization	Procedures without connections	Procedures with connections	Making sense
Connected Learning (Tech)	Antonetti/Stice	Retrieve Copy & paste	Click here, click here, click . . . Prescriptive Learning Accessible Learning	Control- Interests power learning Question, share, contribute, Link, provide feedback	Produce, create Experiment, Design
Academic Strategies*	Similarities and Differences	List facts about A and B	Parallel facts about A and B	Compare or contrast by trait	
	Summarizing/Note-making	Copy	Restate	Personalize or make unique decisions about content	
	Nonlinguistic Representation	Copy other given forms	Place into other forms	Create a new representation	
	Generating/Testing Hypotheses	Copy	Restate "known" pattern	Identify and extend patterns	

(Continued)

FIGURE 2.4 (Continued)

Power Component	1	2	3	4
Personal Response (Clear/Modeled Expectations)	Not necessary	Fill in the blank with "my" answer	Explain and support my ideas (open)	Explain and defend or justify my ideas
Intellectual/Emotional Safety	Not required	Not required	Expression of concepts or recognized patterns	Expression of supported opinions or new ideas
Learning With Others	Take turns talking	Listen and repeat	Interdependence in roles or mini tasks	Interdependence of ideas
Sense of Audience	A partner	The class	An audience I want to appreciate me or my ideas	An audience I want to influence
Novelty and Variety	Recall is fun or different	Product without concepts	Product with concepts	Perspective
Authenticity	Teacher connects to world	Repeat real examples	Recognize real examples	Create real examples
Questions	Closed with single right or wrong answers	Closed but with a "choice" of answers	Open with a range of answers, support, strategies, connections	

*Engaging Qualities***

To provide more clarity, look at the Level 2 indicator for questions. The unstated questions within the task are, "Which right do you understand?" and "How can you draw a picture of that right?" There are five possible answers.

The second part of the task—the collaborative piece—involved the engaging quality Learning With Others. In the sharing activity, your partners had to look at your picture and decide which of the five rights was drawn out. Again, there is a choice of five answers. The cognition continued at a Level 2, but was perhaps made more enjoyable by the "interdependence in roles" between partners. In our video example, the complexity of the drawing actually moved the Learning With Others to "interdependence of ideas" as the partners proposed answers that were logical but unintended. Once again, we see that some students will move a task further across the continua, but the minimum expectation of the collaborative task still forces Learning With Others *across* the rigor divide (Figure 2.5).

FIGURE 2.5 Engaging Qualities of Task #2

Learning With Others	Take turns talking	Listen and repeat	Interdependence in roles or mini tasks	Interdependence of ideas

Tasks #1 and #2 illuminate an interesting data set we find in schools across North America. In our original sample of 17,124 classrooms, we found that 82% of tasks that students perform fall completely to the left of the rigor divide. These tasks require cognition at Level 1 or 2, students do not fully actualize a learning strategy, and the engaging qualities do not cross over the rigor divide. This number often startles teachers when we present it. It is not meant to elicit any particular reaction. It simply is a data point.

As we look further across the data, 12% of student tasks are designed like Task #2: lower levels of cognitive demand—Levels 1 and 2—but with engaging qualities that cross the rigor divide. These activities tend to elicit more energy and enthusiasm from learners because of the engaging qualities, while the thinking remains in the lower levels. Again, there is no judgment against these activities, but we sometimes refer to them as low thinking *with glitter.* Projects, dioramas, PowerPoint presentations, and technology often fall in this category. And as one first-grade teacher tried to convince us, "Glitter works!" It does make accepting meaning more enjoyable.

The remaining 6% of activities we have seen exist fully across the rigor divide. The cognitive demand is Level 3 or 4, the learners have actively used strategies in their cognition, and some combination of engaging qualities designed into the task has brought about the full promise of rigor.

> Don't fall for the common misconception that *everything should be rigorous!*

Teachers often ask us, "What is the best balance between 1s, 2s and 3s/4s?" We don't answer that question early in the trainings, because we don't want educators to start planning how to get to those numbers. We also don't want to lead into the misconception that *everything should be rigorous!* We want to spend more time exploring what each level means and the inherent value of each type of cognition. That said, let's get back to social studies.

Question #3

Do students in our school have a guarantee of these five rights? Use examples to support your response.

Task #3

With your colleagues, share examples from school life of each of the five rights/freedoms in action. (Or give examples of how these rights are not protected in school.)

Record your thoughts here:

After completing the activity, please capture the value of Task #3 on the Task Rubric in Figure 2.6.

In Task #3, we believe the design of the task requires students to make sense and make their own meaning, thus moving the cognition across the rigor divide. In the video example, we hear participants not only talking about the rights, but actually defining the boundaries and limits to the rights. "Yes, students can pray in school, but we don't let them sacrifice animals in the

FIGURE 2.6 Task Rubric for Analysis of Task #3

The "Rigor Divide" (arrow pointing between columns 2 and 3)

	Power Component	1	2	3	4
Cognitive Demand	Bloom – Revised Taxonomy *Examples*	Recall Name the steps	Understand Follow the steps	Apply/Analyze Infer with text support	Evaluate/Create Argue, defend, or justify
	Antonetti/Garver/Stice – Meaning	Repeat accepted meaning	Restate or reproduce accepted meaning	Making meaning: Find patterns Find use for patterns	Compare patterns Add/combine/ignore patterns
	Webb – DOK (Assessment)	Recall	Skill/Concept	Strategic thinking	Extended thinking
	Stein/Smith – Mathematics	Memorization	Procedures without connections	Procedures with connections	Making sense
Connected Learning (Tech)	Antonetti/Stice	Retrieve Copy & paste	Click here, click here, click . . . Prescriptive Learning Accessible Learning	Control- Interests power learning Question, share, contribute, Link, provide feedback	Produce, create Experiment, Design
Academic Strategies*	Similarities and Differences	List facts about A and B	Parallel facts about A and B	Compare or contrast by trait	
	Summarizing/Note-making	Copy	Restate	Personalize or make unique decisions about content	
	Nonlinguistic Representation	Copy other given forms	Place into other forms	Create a new representation	
	Generating/Testing Hypotheses	Copy	Restate "known" pattern	Identify and extend patterns	

(Continued)

FIGURE 2.6 (Continued)

	Power Component	1	2	3	4
Engaging Qualities**	Personal Response (Clear/Modeled Expectations)	Not necessary	Fill in the blank with "my" answer	Explain and support my ideas (open)	Explain and defend or justify my ideas
	Intellectual/Emotional Safety	Not required	Not required	Expression of concepts or recognized patterns	Expression of supported opinions or new ideas
	Learning With Others	Take turns talking	Listen and repeat	Interdependence in roles or mini tasks	Interdependence of ideas
	Sense of Audience	A partner	The class	An audience I want to appreciate me or my ideas	An audience I want to influence
	Novelty and Variety	Recall is fun or different	Product without concepts	Product with concepts	Perspective
	Authenticity	Teacher connects to world	Repeat real examples	Recognize real examples	Create real examples
	Questions	Closed with single right or wrong answers	Closed but with a "choice" of answers	Open with a range of answers, support, strategies, connections	

*The strategies listed are those directly influencing rigor or cognitive demand.

**The engaging quality of choice is not listed; it is effectively provided through choice between rigorous tasks.

online resources

middle of math class." "There are limits to these freedoms and consequences if you cross certain boundaries."

Some learners are making meaning by applying the rights to the familiarity of school, while others may be applying school life to today's content about the First Amendment (application). Still others may be "seeing the rights" in a new light (analysis) or seeing school examples in a new way. In any case, the learners are expressing unique ideas about the rights, not ideas previously stated from a presentation, text, or model. Thus, the task receives a cognitive demand score of Level 3.

We find that teachers and school administrators (and authors of this book) often struggle to differentiate between application and analysis. This is because we do not teach in a vacuum. Some students may sound like they are working at the analysis level, while they are actually just repeating a parent's analysis or the analysis they read from Carl Sagan. When we don't know what understanding the student possessed prior to a task, it makes the naming of the cognition very difficult.

To help clear up this issue, we ask ourselves a series of simple questions. *What was new?* or *What was you?* Did students move the presented content into a new situation or scenario? What ideas did they add to the original content? Did you, the learner, bring your own thoughts into the conversation or commit a new idea to the content? In our video example, we see the learners add the parameters or limits (new) to the school examples. We also hear the "they can, but they can't" conversation as the expression of a new way to think about rights.

When we look at the learners in terms of strategies, we see that the students *personalize or make decisions about content* as they have conversations about the limits or parameters of the rights inside the school. In essence, the learners are summarizing an important content idea about freedoms and rights: They do not exist without responsibility, limits, and consequences.

Another interesting facet of this task is the quality of *authenticity.* As teachers, we can certainly design tasks that have real-world connections, but we cannot decide for our learners whether they will see the tasks as authentic. This task definitely involves the world in which our students live, namely, school. The conversation in this task usually involves real examples from school life, often at a Level 3: *recognizing real examples* of rights, boundaries, and consequences. School may be more real to students than the real world of social studies.

Since the activity surrounding the task was a discussion, we must recognize that it is possible for some students to sit and listen to others without ever committing to a personal response. While many children can learn much in situations such as this, as teachers, we cannot guarantee that the "task predicts performance." For that reason, we must say that the analysis presented on the rubric in Figure 2.7 represents the task for the discussion group, *not* for each individual student.

FIGURE 2.7 Task #3 Analysis

	Power Component	1	2	3	4
Cognitive Demand	Bloom – Revised Taxonomy *Examples*	Recall Name the steps	Understand Follow the steps	Apply/Analyze Infer with text support	Evaluate/Create Argue, defend, or justify
	Antonetti/Garver/Stice – *Meaning*	Repeat accepted meaning	Restate or reproduce accepted meaning	Making meaning: Find patterns Find use for patterns	Compare patterns Add/combine/ignore patterns
	Webb – DOK (Assessment)	Recall	Skill/Concept	Strategic thinking	Extended thinking
	Stein/Smith – Mathematics	Memorization	Procedures without connections	Procedures with connections	Making sense
Connected Learning (Tech)	Antonetti/Stice	Retrieve Copy & paste	Click here, click here, click . . . . Prescriptive Learning Accessible Learning	Control- Interests power learning Question, share, contribute, Link, provide feedback	Produce, create Experiment, Design
Academic Strategies*	Similarities and Differences	List facts about A and B	Parallel facts about A and B	Compare or contrast by trait	
	Summarizing/Note-making	Copy	Restate	Personalize or make unique decisions about content	
	Nonlinguistic Representation	Copy other given forms	Place into other forms	Create a new representation	
	Generating/Testing Hypotheses	Copy	Restate "known" pattern	Identify and extend patterns	

Power Component	1	2	3	4
Personal Response (Clear/Modeled Expectations)	Not necessary	Fill in the blank with "my" answer	Explain and support my ideas (open)	Explain and defend or justify my ideas
Intellectual/Emotional Safety	Not required	Not required	Expression of concepts or recognized patterns	Expression of supported opinions or new ideas
Learning With Others	Take turns talking	Listen and repeat	Interdependence in roles or mini tasks	Interdependence of ideas
Sense of Audience	A partner	The class	An audience I want to appreciate me or my ideas	An audience I want to influence
Novelty and Variety	Recall is fun or different	Product without concepts	Product with concepts	Perspective
Authenticity	Teacher connects to world	Repeat real examples	Recognize real examples	Create real examples
Questions	Closed with single right or wrong answers	Closed but with a "choice" of answers	Open with a range of answers, support, strategies, connections	

*Engaging Qualities***

43

Task #4 requires some additional setup. Our intent with this task design is to land a solid Level 3 across the rigor divide. While the design of the task is collaborative (for the sake of engagement and multiple perspectives), it still might allow some learners to opt out of conversation. With that in mind, we will ask each learner to commit some decision making to paper before entering the conversation. In preparation for this task, consider again the five rights. In the list in Figure 2.8, revise the First Amendment by crossing out and getting rid of any two of the rights. If you are working in a book study or PLC, agree as a group which two rights to delete.

FIGURE 2.8 First Amendment Rights

Cross out two:

Religion
Speech
Press
Assembly
Petition

As we stated, the design intent of this activity is Level 3. Many learners deliberate and agonize over which two they can remove from the list. They actually try to make the task a Level 4 *Evaluate*. To this we say: Stop it! Just cross two off the list so that we can proceed to the real learning task.

As we enter into the heart of Task #4, we want to point out to the readers (and the students in the classroom) that Question #4 is actually the focus of the entire lesson sequence. It serves as the unit's essential question and should be posted in the classroom at this point in the lesson sequence.

Question #4

How do the individual five freedoms of the First Amendment interact to build our version of life in the United States?

Task #4

Look at the list below of historical events, moments, and movements from American history. As you consider each event, decide if the event would have been the same, different, or impossible if the US Constitution guaranteed only your three remaining rights in the First Amendment. Be prepared to explain your thinking.

- Martin Luther King's "I Have a Dream" speech on the National Mall.
- The *Washington Post* uncovering the Watergate scandal.
- Women gaining the right to vote.
- A prayer vigil and protest at the burial of a fallen soldier.
- The creation of a website that details the sources of politicians' campaign contributions.

For a video explanation of the rights outlined in the First Amendment, use the QR code to the companion website at the end of this chapter to view Video 2.4.

If you're ready, you can see the rubric (Figure 2.9) on the following page. How would you "mark" the task?

The responses are now the learner's, crossing the rigor divide in all three domains. There is a sense of "what if" in this task that appeals to many learners and leads to more nuanced understanding of the social studies content as earners generate hypotheses about the impact of removing two rights.

For example, one group of sixth-grade learners argued about the impact on the "I Have a Dream" speech at the National Mall. Ronnie thought that removing free press would not impact King's ability to deliver the speech. Donald agreed but asked, "How would you know about the speech if there was not a press to capture it? We've all seen the videos." Ronnie began to push back, "Well, it could have been told to me by a relative who was there." Donald countered with "Do any of us have relatives who were there?" Ronnie quickly flipped, "You know, I don't think it would have been the same without the press." She continued, "I bet every one of these will be different if all five aren't there. I think life would be very different without all five working together." Bingo! Essential question pay dirt!

It is in this task that we watch many students fully realize working definitions of the five rights. They see the rights or the relationship between the five in a new way that comes from their own analysis. Some participants will argue that this task took them all the way to synthesis or a Level 4. While we do not disagree, we think most learners complete the task through analysis.

You may have already noticed and even wondered why we have not "taught" the learners the definitions of each of the five freedoms. This is not accidental. We would not want to present the definitions and potentially reduce the rigor of Tasks #3 and #4 unless we saw a need to in one of the earlier tasks. While some kids might struggle with the accurate definitions of each of these terms, students typically figure out the definitions as they move through the tasks. It is precisely this struggle that is our goal in the rigorous tasks. An exciting aspect of tasks of rigor is that they provide excellent formative assessment. Throughout the Personal Response moments, learners will share what they know, don't know, and (perhaps more important) what they mis-know. The teacher is free to monitor for misconceptions and then provide necessary guidance and redirection without having to override the task or overteach the content.

> The US Constitution does not have a glossary. The founding fathers had a working vocabulary that has continued to evolve over the past 227 years as the nine justices of the US Supreme Court continue to wrestle with the definitions of these five rights.

For comparison, we have provided our completed rubric in Figure 2.10.

FIGURE 2.9 Task Rubric for Analysis of Task #4

The "Rigor Divide" (arrow pointing between columns 2 and 3)

	Power Component	1	2	3	4
Cognitive Demand	Bloom – Revised Taxonomy *Examples*	Recall; Name the steps	Understand; Follow the steps	Apply/Analyze; Infer with text support	Evaluate/Create; Argue, defend, or justify
	Antonetti/Garver/Stice – Meaning	Repeat accepted meaning	Restate or reproduce accepted meaning	Making meaning: Find patterns; Find use for patterns	Compare patterns; Add/combine/ignore patterns
	Webb – DOK (Assessment)	Recall	Skill/Concept	Strategic thinking	Extended thinking
	Stein/Smith – Mathematics	Memorization	Procedures without connections	Procedures with connections	Making sense
Connected Learning (Tech)	Antonetti/Stice	Retrieve; Copy & paste	Click here, click here, click . . .; Prescriptive Learning; Accessible Learning	Control-; Interests power learning; Question, share, contribute,; Link, provide feedback	Produce, create; Experiment; Design
Academic Strategies*	Similarities and Differences	List facts about A and B	Parallel facts about A and B	Compare or contrast by trait	
	Summarizing/Note-making	Copy	Restate	Personalize or make unique decisions about content	
	Nonlinguistic Representation	Copy other given forms	Place into other forms	Create a new representation	
	Generating/Testing Hypotheses	Copy	Restate "known" pattern	Identify and extend patterns	

Power Component	1	2	3	4
Personal Response (Clear/Modeled Expectations)	Not necessary	Fill in the blank with "my" answer	Explain and support my ideas (open)	Explain and defend or justify my ideas
Intellectual/Emotional Safety	Not required	Not required	Expression of concepts or recognized patterns	Expression of supported opinions or new ideas
Learning With Others	Take turns talking	Listen and repeat	Interdependence in roles or mini tasks	Interdependence of ideas
Sense of Audience	A partner	The class	An audience I want to appreciate me or my ideas	An audience I want to influence
Novelty and Variety	Recall is fun or different	Product without concepts	Product with concepts	Perspective
Authenticity	Teacher connects to world	Repeat real examples	Recognize real examples	Create real examples
Questions	Closed with single right or wrong answers	Closed but with a "choice" of answers	Open with a range of answers, support, strategies, connections	

Engaging Qualities**

*The strategies listed are those directly influencing rigor or cognitive demand.

**The engaging quality of choice is not listed; it is effectively provided through choice between rigorous tasks.

online resources

FIGURE 2.10 Task #4 Analysis by John and Terri

	Power Component	1	2	3	4
Cognitive Demand	Bloom – Revised Taxonomy *Examples*	Recall Name the steps	Understand Follow the steps	Apply/Analyze Infer with text support	Evaluate/Create Argue, defend, or justify
	Antonetti/Garver/Stice – Meaning	Repeat accepted meaning	Restate or reproduce accepted meaning	Making meaning: Find patterns Find use for patterns	Compare patterns Add/combine/ignore patterns
	Webb – DOK (Assessment)	Recall	Skill/Concept	Strategic thinking	Extended thinking
	Stein/Smith – Mathematics	Memorization	Procedures without connections	Procedures with connections	Making sense
Connected Learning (Tech)	Antonetti/Stice	Retrieve Copy & paste	Click here, click here, click… Prescriptive Learning Accessible Learning	Control- Interests power learning Question, share, contribute, Link, provide feedback	Produce, create Experiment, Design
Academic Strategies*	Similarities and Differences	List facts about A and B	Parallel facts about A and B	Compare or contrast by trait	
	Summarizing/Note-making	Copy	Restate	Personalize or make unique decisions about content	
	Nonlinguistic Representation	Copy other given forms	Place into other forms	Create a new representation	
	Generating/Testing Hypotheses	Copy	Restate "known" pattern	Identify and extend patterns	

Power Component	1	2	3	4
Personal Response (Clear/Modeled Expectations)	Not necessary	Fill in the blank with "my" answer	Explain and support my ideas (open)	Explain and defend or justify my ideas
Intellectual/Emotional Safety	Not required	Not required	Expression of concepts or recognized patterns	Expression of supported opinions or new ideas
Learning With Others	Take turns talking	Listen and repeat	Interdependence in roles or mini tasks	Interdependence of ideas
Sense of Audience	A partner	The class	An audience I want to appreciate me or my ideas	An audience I want to influence
Novelty and Variety	Recall is fun or different	Product without concepts	Product with concepts	Perspective
Authenticity	Teacher connects to world	Repeat real examples	Recognize real examples	Create real examples
Questions	Closed with single right or wrong answers	Closed but with a "choice" of answers	Open with a range of answers, support, strategies, connections	

*Engaging Qualities***

49

> ## Question #5
>
> Which of the five freedoms is the most important? Why?
>
> ## Task #5
>
> Working with your colleagues, come to consensus and place the five rights on the continuum in Figure 2.11 in order from least important to most important. Be prepared to explain your thinking process and your final product.

FIGURE 2.11 Continuum for Placement of Rights

Ready. You know the drill. Use the rubric in Figure 2.12.

When we do this task live with students or with adults, it is interesting to watch the table groups decide how to approach the work. Whether they recognize it or not, most teams quickly consider the engaging quality of Intellectual/Emotional Safety. They wrestle with how each of their voices will be heard. Will there be a dominant voice that pushes consensus in a particular direction?

Oftentimes, a member of the group will suggest "Let's all write down our own thoughts first and then compare and try to come to consensus." As teachers, we are always so excited when this occurs naturally. The group has self-imposed the Personal Response quality of engagement, as well as a guarantee of individual cognitive demand, and we see the energy and commitment increase for each member of that group as they move into Learning With Others.

Regardless of the placement of the five rights, the group must work through a cognitive demand at Level 4, *evaluate*. By definition, evaluation is the determination that something has more value than something else. Some learners use a strategy of *compare or contrast by trait* as they consider two rights at a time—for example, which is more important, religion or speech? As they continue this strategy, they may make comparisons at least four times to place the rights on the continuum. Others go straight to *personalize or make unique decisions about content*: "Speech is the most important because all of the others are predicated upon it."

Still others operate by moving the cognition to *create* as they articulate ideas such as, "In today's world with technology, speech and press are now one and the same." We will discuss creativity more in Chapter 5, but for now we

FIGURE 2.12 Task Rubric for Analysis of Task #5

	Power Component	1	2	3	4
Cognitive Demand	Bloom – Revised Taxonomy *Examples*	Recall Name the steps	Understand Follow the steps	Apply/Analyze Infer with text support	Evaluate/Create Argue, defend, or justify
	Antonetti/Garver/Stice – Meaning	Repeat accepted meaning	Restate or reproduce accepted meaning	Making meaning: Find patterns Find use for patterns	Compare patterns Add/combine/ignore patterns
	Webb – DOK (Assessment)	Recall	Skill/Concept	Strategic thinking	Extended thinking
	Stein/Smith – Mathematics	Memorization	Procedures without connections	Procedures with connections	Making sense
Connected Learning (Tech)	Antonetti/Stice	Retrieve Copy & paste	Click here, click here, click . . . Prescriptive Learning Accessible Learning	Control- Interests power learning Question, share, contribute, Link, provide feedback	Produce, create Experiment Design
Academic Strategies*	Similarities and Differences	List facts about A and B	Parallel facts about A and B	Compare or contrast by trait	
	Summarizing/Note-making	Copy	Restate	Personalize or make unique decisions about content	
	Nonlinguistic Representation	Copy other given forms	Place into other forms	Create a new representation	
	Generating/Testing Hypotheses	Copy	Restate "known" pattern	Identify and extend patterns	

(Continued)

FIGURE 2.12 (Continued)

Power Component	1	2	3	4
Engaging Qualities*				
Personal Response (Clear/Modeled Expectations)	Not necessary	Fill in the blank with "my" answer	Explain and support my ideas (open)	Explain and defend or justify my ideas
Intellectual/Emotional Safety	Not required	Not required	Expression of concepts or recognized patterns	Expression of supported opinions or new ideas
Learning With Others	Take turns talking	Listen and repeat	Interdependence in roles or mini tasks	Interdependence of ideas
Sense of Audience	A partner	The class	An audience I want to appreciate me or my ideas	An audience I want to influence
Novelty and Variety	Recall is fun or different	Product without concepts	Product with concepts	Perspective
Authenticity	Teacher connects to world	Repeat real examples	Recognize real examples	Create real examples
Questions	Closed with single right or wrong answers	Closed but with a "choice" of answers	Open with a range of answers, support, strategies, connections	

*The strategies listed are those directly influencing rigor or cognitive demand.

**The engaging quality of choice is not listed; it is effectively provided through choice between rigorous tasks.

online resources

can describe this thinking as a form of *create* when the learner combines ideas and patterns into new ideas.

When the group comes together to build consensus, it is interesting to see which learners run with the quality of Sense of Audience that is in the collaborative task as they try to *influence* their audience of peers and convince them of the "right-est" answer.

So, our final rubric annotation is shown in Figure 2.13.

WHERE WAS THE POWER?

Now that we have completed five distinctly different learning tasks for the First Amendment, we would propose two final reflective questions of Personal Response. There are no wrong answers!

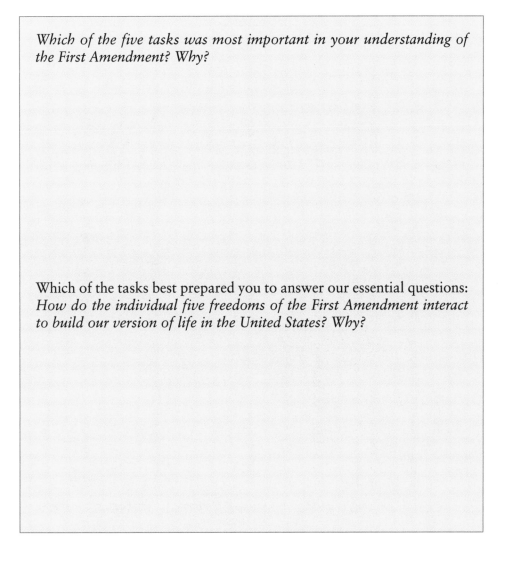

Which of the five tasks was most important in your understanding of the First Amendment? Why?

Which of the tasks best prepared you to answer our essential questions: *How do the individual five freedoms of the First Amendment interact to build our version of life in the United States? Why?*

FIGURE 2.13 Task #5 Analysis

	Power Component	1	2	3	4
Cognitive Demand	Bloom – Revised Taxonomy *Examples*	Recall Name the steps	Understand Follow the steps	Apply/Analyze Infer with text support	(Evaluate)/Create Argue, defend, or justify
	Antonetti/Garver/Stice – Meaning	Repeat accepted meaning	Restate or reproduce accepted meaning	Making meaning: Find patterns Find use for patterns	Compare patterns Add/combine/ignore patterns
	Webb – DOK (Assessment)	Recall	Skill/Concept	Strategic thinking	Extended thinking
	Stein/Smith – Mathematics	Memorization	Procedures without connections	Procedures with connections	Making sense
Connected Learning (Tech)	Antonetti/Stice	Retrieve Copy & paste	Click here, click here, click . . . Prescriptive Learning Accessible Learning	Control- Interests power learning Question, share, contribute, Link, provide feedback	Produce, create Experiment, Design
Academic Strategies*	Similarities and Differences	List facts about A and B	Parallel facts about A and B	Compare or contrast by trait	
	Summarizing/Note-making	Copy	Restate	Personalize or make unique decisions about content	
	Nonlinguistic Representation	Copy other given forms	Place into other forms	Create a new representation	
	Generating/Testing Hypotheses	Copy	Restate "known" pattern	Identify and extend patterns	

Power Component	1	2	3	4
Personal Response (Clear/Modeled Expectations)	Not necessary	Fill in the blank with "my" answer	Explain and support my ideas (open)	Explain and defend or justify my ideas
Intellectual/Emotional Safety	Not required	Not required	Expression of concepts or recognized patterns	Expression of supported opinions or new ideas
Learning With Others	Take turns talking	Listen and repeat	Interdependence in roles or mini tasks	Interdependence of ideas
Sense of Audience	A partner	The class	An audience I want to appreciate me or my ideas*	An audience I want to influence
Novelty and Variety	Recall is fun or different	Product without concepts	Product with concepts	Perspective
Authenticity	Teacher connects to world	Repeat real examples	Recognize real examples	Create real examples
Questions	Closed with single right or wrong answers	Closed but with a "choice" of answers	Open with a range of answers, support, strategies, connections	

*Engaging Qualities***

Each of the tasks in the sequence serves a particular purpose—there is no "weak" task. If the task gets the learners where we need them, the task is powerful in its own way. In this particular sequence, the tasks probably can not be used out of order. Obviously, the sequence of tasks begins with locating the five rights. Without the retrieval of content in Task #1, the rest of the lesson would not be possible.

Task #2 is often a favorite of learners, but teachers are sometimes unwilling to articulate this as the most important in their learning because they don't want to say that a Level 2 cognitive demand might be more important to them than a Level 3 or Level 4. We must get past this temptation to think that one task has more value to a class than another (even as we ask you to articulate which was the most important). Task #2 plays a very important role in the scope and sequence of this lesson. Although it is just shy of crossing into rigor, it provides learners with a chance to be successful without taking a big intellectual risk.

Tasks #3, # 4, and #5 all cross the rigor divide but provide different entry points, strategies, and engaging qualities. Most learners have a strong connection to one of these tasks for a wide variety of reasons.

In our never-ending quest to find balance in our classrooms, we must recognize the value of each of the tasks as well as the purpose of each of the tasks. And we must return to the learning objective or goals to determine the impact of the tasks on the learning. We could say that three of the five tasks were rigorous. That's a rigor quotient of 60%. While it is impressive, our research suggests a level that high is not necessary for optimal learning as we balance effective learning and efficient teaching. We might have the same level of success with our students if we did Tasks #1 and #2, and then let students choose among the remaining three tasks. That would still give us a rigor quotient of 33%, if we think of it as one out of three tasks, or a rigor quotient of 40% if we consider the amount of time spent across the three tasks.

With the exception of Task #1, technology did not play a role in our work or discussion in this chapter. We will bring technology in as we move through the book. There's no need for technology until we are confident in our planning with the other design components.

http://resources.corwin.com/powerfultask

CHAPTER 3

The Power of Engagement

How important is student engagement to the learning process? Charlotte Danielson writes in her *Enhancing Professional Practice: A Framework for Teaching*, that without student engagement, nothing else done will matter. Student engagement is not always about hands-on actions; it is not about busy work. Intellectual involvement is the definition of true engagement (Danielson, 2007, pp. 82–85).

As we looked for student engagement in classrooms, we had to recognize and articulate the distinctions among volunteerism, participation, and true engagement. Individual volunteerism begins on the kindergarten carpet and continues to be a part of the overwhelming majority of classrooms we visit: Most classrooms have a sufficient number of students willing to raise their hands and interact during teacher-directed activities. We sometimes refer to this phenomenon as "instructional volleyball." The teacher serves up a question, and the first volunteer returns an answer, sometimes with an assist from another learner. The teacher again takes control of the game and serves to another learner, inviting him to play, while many other students remain "on the bench." Regardless of the energy provide by volunteers, participation by all students is optional.

As teachers require all students to do the work and the invitation becomes an expectation for all students, volunteerism gives way to participation. Again, our visits continue to present some interesting trends: Students typically perform the work they are given and remain compliantly on task. Although students respond to tasks with a range of energies—from minimal expenditure to enthusiastic compliance, participation is often more closely related to motivation than it is to engagement. Whether students do it to please the teacher, to do the right thing, or to avoid negative consequences, participation does not seem to be a problem in the vast majority of classrooms we visit.

For our work, we use two definitions of learner engagement with an important distinction between the two:

> engagement: when the work has meaning to the learner
>
> cognitive engagement: when the learner *makes* meaning

We might even consider a continuum of engagement in a required task:

participation……………..engagement………………..cognitive engagement

Let's consider three students preparing for the mandatory middle school science fair.

Student #1 Participates

Neal does not even choose an investigation until the day before the assignment is due. He jumps online and finds a canned project that can be completed in a single hour. (Seriously, the website is https://goo.gl/vbbGFQ; you can also find the link on the companion website.)

He follows the procedures and steps as outlined on the website and ends up with a completed project at 11:59 p.m.

Student #2 Engages

On Tuesday, Mattie searches Pinterest and finds a fabulous backdrop for a project about determining which brand of popcorn pops best. She searches a second website and finds a step-by-step protocol with the procedures already written up and downloadable. On Wednesday, she buys the popcorn and completes the investigation. Thursday and Friday evenings—and a large part of Saturday—are dedicated to making the backdrop. Mattie returns from the local movie theatre and uses popcorn containers to jazz up the board. She installs Christmas lights through the back side of the board to make a movie marquee with running, twinkling lights. Visually, the board is stunning. To appeal to the judges' other senses, Mattie downloads an MP3 audio file of popcorn popping which she plays on a continuous loop on her iPhone. Finally, from Amazon.com, she orders popcorn-scented wax melts to provide a mouth-watering experience for the science fair guests.

Student #3 Engages Cognitively

Kaitlyn was struggling to come up with an idea for her science fair investigation. While she was babysitting for a neighbor on a Friday night, eight-month-old Thomas provided inspiration when his diaper proved to be less absorbent than it needed to be. As she sat rocking Thomas back to sleep, Kaitlyn's mind began to ask questions. Were some diapers more absorbent than others? What were the materials in diapers that absorbed the most liquid? Could diapers absorb liquid but still leave moisture touching the baby's skin? Did babies who wore "better" diapers cry less and end up staying in a wet diaper longer than babies in cheap diapers? Which is the most important consideration in buying diapers?

As we consider the three approaches to the science fair project, we can see the continuum of engagement. Neal is all about efficiency. An hour of participation in following someone else's plan and he is finished. Mattie engages deeply in the presentation, the drama, and the sense of audience. She enjoys the artistic nature of the work and finds meaning in the aesthetics of this part of the project. She is certainly cognitive and creative, but the energy goes into the backdrop, not the science. It is Kaitlyn who is cognitively engaged as she begins to make meaning. It is this small moment of cognition that is perhaps one of the most important learning objectives of the assignment.

Let's look at another scenario in which technology plays a role in moving the continuum of engagement.

Mrs. Mills is preparing her students for a new math problem and focuses her young learners up front by saying, "We are going to work a problem, but in this problem, I am more interested in seeing the strategy you use to solve it than the right answer to the problem." The teacher presents the story problem:

> Five students are dressing up as Scooby Doo for our Halloween party. They each will eat three Scooby Doo snacks. How many Scooby Doo snacks does the teacher need to buy for the party?

Miss Mills instructs her students, "Show your work. Use the strategy that makes the most sense to you and solves the problem."

The students get to work. As Mrs. Mills walks around the room, she observes a variety of strategies being used to find the answer to the problem. After a few minutes, she says, "Freeze." The students stop, and Mrs. Mills selects students representing a variety of strategies, and asks them to share their thinking with their classmates via the document camera.

Next, Mrs. Mills asks those students still seated to stand and join the classmate who shared a strategy that makes the most sense to them. Using this "choose your strategy" structure, Mrs. Mills allows the students to find one of many entry points into the mathematical thinking. In their small groups, the students finish solving the problem together. Some of the strategies utilized by the learners are shown below.

Later in the week, the students used an online video creation tool (www .animoto.com) to make the videos (products) that showed their work. The

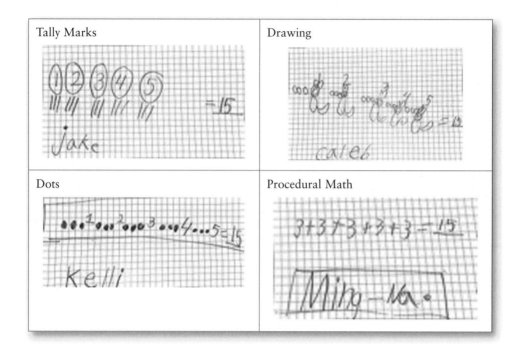

Tally Marks	Drawing
① ② ③ ④ ⑤ = 15 Jake	... = 12 caleb
Dots	**Procedural Math**
●●●1 ●●●2 ●●●3 ●●●4 ...5 = 15 Kelli	$3+3+3+3+3 = 15$ Ming - Na

videos were shared on the class website and shared with the community, family, and friends.

THE QUALITIES OF ENGAGEMENT

Please label the design qualities on the band of the Task Rubric shown in Figure 3.1 that make this an engaging task.

Using the Powerful Task Rubric, let's take a moment to analyze this task through the component of engaging qualities. If we consider the continuum of Personal Response, this task is best described by the Level 3 indicator *explain and support my ideas*. All students are given the same math problem and are encouraged to solve it with the strategy that makes sense to them. The students had individual thoughts about how to solve the problem. It is important to note, while the problem had only one correct answer, it had multiple ways it could be solved.

In this task, Mrs. Mills clearly explains to her students, "I am more interested in seeing the strategy you use to solve the problem, more than the right answer to the problem." Her comment builds a sense of Intellectual/Emotional Safety for her students, because now her students are likely comfortable to take a risk and try to solve the problem in any way that they are able to make sense. In other words, they are able to *recognize and express concepts* (Level 3 indicator).

The second part of the task (forming groups to create a video product) is based on Learning With Others. The video product requires each group of

FIGURE 3.1 Engaging Qualities Component of Task Rubric for Analysis

Engaging Qualities**					
	Personal Response (Clear/Modeled Expectations)	Not necessary	Fill in the blank with "my" answer	Explain and support my ideas (open)	Explain and defend or justify my ideas
	Intellectual/ Emotional Safety	Not required	Not required	Expression of concepts or recognized patterns	Expression of supported opinions or new ideas
	Learning With Others	Take turns talking	Listen and repeat	Interdependence in roles or mini task	Interdependence of ideas
	Sense of Audience	A partner	The class	An audience I want to appreciate me or my ideas	An audience I want to influence
	Novelty and Variety	Recall is fun or different	Product without concepts	Product with concepts	Perspective
	Authenticity	Teacher connects to world	Repeat real examples	Recognize real examples	Create real examples

students to *interdependently take on a role* (Level 3 indicator) and together complete the task of creating a video that demonstrates their solution. For example, Ronan may have chosen the music, while Michael decided on the background graphic.

In the original math problem, Mrs. Mills guaranteed Personal Response in the task before allowing the Learning With Others. As each student moved to join the different strategy groups, she could choose to meet up with others who used the same strategy or join a group that used a different strategy that made "even more sense" than her original approach. Thus, the combination of Personal Response and Learning With Others took the Intellectual/Emotional Safety to a more powerful level.

For students in first grade, there is probably a strong Sense of Audience. With the video being posted on the classroom website, Grandma and Grandpa, as well as Mom and Dad, will see their work. Most learners greatly *value the opinion of those they care about the most*

Learning With Others

In the classrooms we visit, we see teachers across the country utilizing cooperative learning structures. Sometimes we want these structures to simply build collaboration and sense of community—we all contribute and we all listen. Other times, the focus of the cooperative learning is to allow (or force) everyone to contribute ideas to the task—as in group brainstorming. At the most powerful implementation, the Level 4 indicator of this quality is interdependence of ideas. At this level, learners compare, argue, combine, and massage ideas into a group consensus. While all of these purposes are valid and important in the classroom, we must make sure the collaborative structure and the collaborative task both serve our intent.

(Level 3 indicator) and often are more attentive to their work because of the elevated level of concern.

In this task, the Novelty and Variety of the video work grabbed the students' attention because of both the process and product. The video requirement in the task was the first time students used Animoto. Using technology in a task such as this can present an interesting risk: It can shift the students' attention from thinking and learning to the fun and newness of the activity. Like many teachers, however, we have often found the risk pays off.

The student work in this task demonstrates some Authenticity. Mrs. Mills has taken a very real situation in the life of a first grader (attending a Halloween party) and connected it to a lesson on mathematics. In this case, the authenticity remains, perhaps, at the teacher-control level.

In the inspection of the student work Mrs. Mills' task requires of her students, we are able to find several engaging qualities (Figure 3.2).

What is most engaging in the task wins!

The bottom line is this: What is most engaging in the task wins!

Another scenario we occasionally see when teachers are focused on making content more engaging is the use of a "project menu." Instead of students using a traditional method with paper and pencil to demonstrate their learning, they are given a menu of projects with options of products that they may produce. Using the QR code at the end of the chapter, or by going onto the companion website, let's look at several classroom examples to see what these projects might look like.

In Mrs. Shirley's second- and third-grade classroom, students are provided a custom project menu to determine how they will demonstrate their knowledge level of the content. For example, Mattie decides to make an informational video about volcanoes, while Reid constructs a physical model of Diamond Head, a volcanic tuff cone on the Hawaiian island. Both products provide opportunities for the students to take their learning far beyond the standards' requirements. When we look at the products through the lens of the engaging qualities, Mattie's movie clip has evidence of Personal Response as she is *explaining her ideas* about volcanoes and *supporting them visually, textually, and auditorily*. On the other hand, when we look at Reid's model of Diamond Head, we are limited to only what we see visually. His product depends heavily upon the details he purposefully adds to his model to show what he knows about the volcanic tuff cone. We are able to see the same level of Personal Response in his model as we are in Mattie's movie, *explanation of ideas with supporting details*. Both Mattie's and Reid's products were produced with a Sense of Audience in mind. The students in Mrs. Shirley's class know she schedules the presentations of products at a convenient time for their family, friends, and community members to attend. Like both the

FIGURE 3.2 Engaging Qualities Rubric Analysis for Scooby DOO Task

	Power Component	1	2	3	4
Cognitive Demand	Bloom—Revised Taxonomy *Examples*	Recall / Name the steps	Understand / Follow the steps	Apply/Analyze / Infer with text support	Evaluate/Create / Argue, defend, or justify
Cognitive Demand	Antonetti/GarverfStice— Meaning	Repeat accepted meaning	Restate or reproduce accepted meaning	Making meaning: Find patterns / Find use for patterns	Compare patterns / Add/combine/ignore patterns
Cognitive Demand	Webb—DOK (Assessment)	Recall	Skill/Concept	Strategic thinking	Extended thinking
Cognitive Demand	Stein/Smith—Mathematics	Memorization	Procedures without connections	Procedures with connections	(Making sense)
Connected Learning (Tech)	Antonetti/Stice	Retrieve / Copy & paste	Click here, click here, click … / Prescriptive Learning / Accessible Learning	Control- / Interests power learning / Question, share, contribute, / Link, provide feedback	
Academic Strategies*	Similarities and Differences	List facts about A and B	Parallel facts about A and B	Compare or contrast by trait	
Academic Strategies*	Summarizing/Note-making	Copy	Restate	(Personalize) or make unique decisions about content	
Academic Strategies*	Nonlinguistic Representation	Copy other given forms	Place into other forms	Create a new representation	
Academic Strategies*	Generating/Testing Hypotheses	Copy	Restate "known" pattern	Identify and extend patterns	
Engaging Qualities**	PersonalResponse (Clear/Modeled Expectations)	Not necessary	Fill in the blank with "my" answer	(Explain and support as open)	(Explain and defend or justify my ideas)
Engaging Qualities**	Intellectual/Emotional Safety	Not required	Not required	Expression of concepts or recognized patterns	(Expression of supported opinions or new ideas)
Engaging Qualities**	Learning With Others	Take turns talking	Listen and repeat	Interdependence in roles or mini tasks	(Interdependence of ideas)
Engaging Qualities**	Sense of Audience	A partner	The class	An audience I want to appreciate me or my ideas*	An audience I want to influence
Engaging Qualities**	Novelty and Variety	Recall is fun or different	Product without concepts	Product with concepts	(Perspective)
Engaging Qualities**	Authenticity	Teacher connects to world	Repeat real examples	Recognize real examples	Create real examples
Engaging Qualities**	Questions	Closed with single right or wrong answers	Closed but with a "choice" of answers	(Open with a range of answers, support, connections)	Open with a range of answers, support, strategies, connections

science fair products, and Mrs. Mills's Scooby Doo products, Mrs. Shirley's project menu approach has engaging qualities as well. What we know about highly engaging tasks is most students want to do them simply because they make learning seem like a fun thing to do.

As you continue to play with the rubric, you may have to adjust your thinking. We provide our thoughts about the placement and the power of a task, but you may see the task differently. This is actually the beauty of the tool: It allows us as professionals to have conversations about task design and task implementation. It's not about the "right" answer on the rubric, it's about the kind of thinking we want to add to our design process as teachers.

As authors, from the first day our two worlds met, we knew there was a solid connection between the engagement framework and the world of the digital revolution. Yet we had to merge our Personal Response with some Learning With Others. The Comparison of Similarities table (Figure 3.3) shows how we each saw the qualities.

INTERACTION AS ENGAGEMENT

And so in our journey together we began trying to make sense of what we both knew—that technology does bring engaging qualities to a task. The Instructional Core reminds us that learners must interact with the content. Technology can play a significant role between the student and the content. It can quickly grab the learner's attention and then provide moments of making sense and constructing meaning. Debra Pickering once described this role by saying "technologies enhance and expand student interactions." In essence she was saying that when we interface with technology, we begin to make sense through one of four domains:

(1) visual interaction

(2) physical interaction

(3) social interaction

(4) cognitive interaction

Learners are in the first domain, visual interaction, when they are seeking information and making meaning of it. While our other senses are important in learning, molecular biologist John Medina (2014) suggests that "vision trumps all other senses" (p. 240). As we read a passage or listen to a master storyteller, we must visualize the content or play a movie in our mind. A concept does not become clear to most of us until we see it take different forms. Teachers have long known the power of the illustration, the photograph, the actual frog dissection to make learning come alive. Does a technology-rich environment amplify visual interactions? Absolutely! We see this all of the time as we visually interact with content. Sometimes it can arrive in a text

FIGURE 3.3 Comparison of Similarities

Engaging Quality	John's World of Engagement	Terri's World of the Digital Revolution
Personal Response	The work allows me to react and have my own, unique thoughts based upon my schema. Consequently, there is more than one answer.	Social media are digital tools that allow me to react and express my ideas, notions, opinions, views, impressions, feelings, or judgments with an audience in one click.
Clear/Modeled Expectations	I know what success looks like; it may have been modeled for me. I know the criteria for my personal response.	YouTube is an excellent resource for learning through clear/modeled steps and examples of success.
Intellectual/ Emotional Safety	I am comfortable taking risks. It is okay to have a different answer or to be wrong on the way to be being right.	Response tools such as Poll Everywhere and Today's Meet allow me to share my thinking without others laughing at what I might say.
Learning With Others	I have the opportunity to interact with others, sharing and analyzing my ideas and theirs. My learning is different because of this process.	Web 2.0 tools such as Google Apps are designed specifically for Learning With Others opportunities!
Sense of Audience	Someone whose opinion I care about is going to see my work. I'll be more attentive to my work because of an elevated level of concern.	The Web 2.0 movement is all about moving users of the Web from being passive consumers of media to contributors using digital tools to create and share their knowledge with others.
Choice	I get to choose how I am going to gain information or knowledge or how I will demonstrate my learning. I have some control over my work.	The Internet brings choice to life for every learner. Learning in a connected environment makes personalized learning possible. With a plethora of digital tools available to demonstrate learning, as well as an abundance of curated links to explore any topic of interest, choice is at the heart of personalized learning.
Novelty and Variety	The work grabs my attention because it is new and different. It may be different in procedure, product, perspective, or place.	Living in "an app for that" world reminds us there is an app for nearly everything! Using apps to create videos, podcasts, images, memes, polls, and quizzes to grab learners' attention has never been easier.
Authenticity	I understand that real people need to know how to do this work. I see connections to my world or the world at large.	The Internet allows every learner to connect and extend the four walls of the classroom to include experts and people from all over the world.

in the form of an emoji, while at other times it could be through drawings, charts, graphs, images, videos, or maps. Online content can provide a richness in visual experiences through websites, browsers, and search engine images. Content is also accessible through multiple modalities like virtual reality headsets, Google Cardboard, social media, desktops, laptops, and even the mobile devices we carry in our pockets.

Learners are in the second domain, physical interaction, when they are using physical motions and activities during the learning process. Does a technology-rich environment amplify physical engagement? Definitely! When learners physically engage with a device by interacting through the act of drawing, writing, keyboarding, tapping, touching, pinching, or pulling various objects, it brings an entirely new experience to a learning environment. At this particular time perhaps the strongest example of physical interaction is fitness/activity trackers. According to the International Data Corporation, in 2015, 78.1 million fitness trackers were shipped to users around the globe. All of a sudden, users could sync data to their computers or phones and get real-time measurements of steps taken, miles walked, and calories burned as well as track vital signs and sleep patterns. Taking advantage of a technology-rich environment seems to make people more inspired and motivated to physically engage in an attempt to live healthier lifestyles.

Learners are in the third domain, social interaction, when they are interacting with others in a variety of ways. Does a technology-rich environment amplify social engagement? It must; otherwise, how do you explain the fact that approximately two thirds of all Americans have a profile on social media and check for updates on their feed an average of 5.6 times per day? Furthermore, how do we explain that Facebook's population is now as large as that of the world's largest country, with 1.13 billion daily active users? Taking advantage of a technology-rich environment allows opportunities to make the world more open and connected through social engagement, interacting and participating in the lives of a variety of people whom we may never meet face-to-face.

The fourth domain, cognitive interaction, is the most important to educators, because we want our students thinking, plus we want evidence to know how they are thinking. For example, when learners are cognitively engaged, they might be applying, analyzing, inferring, evaluating, arguing, defending, proving, or justifying their thinking. Simply put, cognitive engagement occurs when learners make meaning rather than accept another's thinking. Does a technology-rich environment amplify cognitive engagement? Indeed! Learners who thrive in a connected world control their depth of understanding as well as the level of cognitive complexity. Connected learners gain knowledge from multiple perspectives, and experience presentations through a variety of modalities, all of which require cognitive engagement to solve problems and interact with content. As leaders of learning, cognitive engagement is our goal; physical and social engagement serve to support that goal. Categories of engagement may intertwine—that is, thoughtful educators may purposefully design tasks for students to be physically, socially, and cognitively engaging.

On April 3, 2010, Apple launched the sale of the iPad, a revolutionary device for browsing the web, enjoying photos, watching videos, listening to music, playing games, reading e-books, and much more. Terri still recalls the "wow factor" experience of visual and physical interactions with the device. With over 140,000 apps available a tap away, she knew the potential was there for cognitive interactions as well.

As it turns out, the iPad was the perfect birthday gift for Terri's four-year-old granddaughter. Terri carefully selected each app for the device, ensuring opportunities for cognitive engagement were there. As one might predict, it was only a matter of time until Gracie purchased other apps. Cupcake Maker, created by Sunstorm Interactive, was one of those apps. It is designed to allow the user to experience making cupcakes virtually. From gathering the ingredients to gobbling up the tasty treats, it all happens with physical interactions. Dragging, pinching, pulling, and tapping the screen, the user is mixing, baking, and eating cupcakes. Gracie loved making cupcakes with her app! On the other hand, Terri was a bit disappointed with Gracie's obsession because, at first glance, it appeared the experience was limited to visual and physical interactions. Terri wanted more. She wanted to know some thinking/cognitive interaction was happening as well.

While riding in the car one day, Gracie asked if she could make real cupcakes when they got home. She began to spell out the process. "I will get the ingredients together. I know everything we need: vegetable oil, vanilla flavoring, baking powder, eggs." Undeniably, the four-year-old was recalling facts she had learned from the app. As she began the process of making the cupcakes, it soon became apparent she knew the entire process, including the sequence of events (mixing ingredients, pouring batter into cupcake holders, baking, etc.). The Cupcake Maker app offered visual, physical, and cognitive interactions.

Let's pause for a moment and inspect the engaging qualities of Gracie's task (Figure 3.4).

- The task clearly demonstrates Authenticity, but only because Gracie chooses to take it there when she asks if she can make "real cupcakes" or *create real examples*.

- Gracie has a sense of Personal Response in her work—she is selecting and choosing what she wants to *fill in the blank* (sprinkles, colors of icing, various toppings, etc.) as she makes her cupcake.

- For a young learner like Gracie, there is almost always a Sense of Audience—she always wants *an audience to appreciate* her.

- By design, the app brings Novelty and Variety—every time Gracie launches the app, she creates a new *product without concepts*, meaning she uses very little thinking about what she is creating, because the focus of her task is to have fun!

FIGURE 3.4 Engaging Qualities of Gracie's Task

Engaging Qualities**	Personal Response (Clear/ Modeled Expectations)	Not necessary	Fill in the blank with "my" answer	Explain and support my ideas (open)	Explain and defend or justify my ideas
	Intellectual/ Emotional Safety	Not required	Not required	Expression of concepts or recognized patterns	Expression of supported opinions or new ideas
	Learning With Others	Take turns talking	Listen and repeat	Interdependence in roles or mini tasks	Interdependence of ideas
	Sense of Audience	A partner	The class	An audience I want to appreciate me or my ideas	An audience I want to influence
	Novelty and Variety	Recall is fun or different	Product without concepts	Product with concepts	Perspective
	Authenticity	Teacher connects to world	Repeat real examples	Recognize real examples	Create real examples

A TASK IS POWERED UP

Flash forward a year later; Gracie is five years old and still enjoying interactive play with the Cupcake App. Obviously, at this point of interacting with the app, there is less cognitive interaction going on, so Terri decides to change the task for the Cupcake Maker. In the Van de Walle Professional Mathematics Series, *Teaching Student-Centered Mathematics,* John Van de Walle writes

> The first goal in the development of fractions should be to help children construct the idea of fractional parts of the whole—the parts that result when the whole or unit has been partitioned into equal-sized portions or fair shares. Children seem to understand the idea of separating a quantity into two or more parts to be shared fairly among friends. (2006, p. 252)

With the Van de Walle theory in mind, Terri reminds Gracie of one of her favorite stories, *The Doorbell Rang,* by Pat Hutchins, which is a story about a mom baking cookies. With each ring of the doorbell more friends come to share the cookies and everyone gets fair shares. Terri explains to Gracie,

"Just like in the story, when you hear the doorbell ring, I will tell you who is at the door, and you will need to share the cupcakes you are making with Cupcake Maker fairly."

The difficulty level of the task was determined by the relationship between the number of things to be shared and the number of people to in which to share it. Early on, Gracie grasped the concept of sharing wholes as well as halving, and we kept the numbers even (2, 4, 6, 8). Gradually, we increased the difficulty level and challenged her to share 6 cupcakes among 5 friends, stressing everyone must have a fair share.

> Gracie's favorite app became Explain Everything because, she said, "It makes me feel like a teacher when I am explaining everything!" When learners invest energy into a task and experience validation, they want to go again, even when the task is challenging.

Through a little app smashing (using multiple apps in conjunction with one another to complete a final task), Gracie was able to capture a picture of cupcakes she created with the Cupcake Maker app. Next, she

> A rigorous task is not a powerful task if the learners do not *want* to do it.

launched the Explain Everything app, which is an interactive whiteboard/screencasting app that let Gracie annotate and record her voice explaining her thoughts.

During this learning experience, Terri never used the word *fraction* when discussing the work Gracie was doing; however, it was evident this five-year-old was beginning to develop knowledge and understanding of fractions! Flash forward three years, and Gracie is now in third grade, where formal instruction with fraction concepts begin. As the teacher introduces the term *fraction* and defines it as part of the whole, Gracie makes the connection between the teacher's definition and the Cupcake Maker experience. Scan the QR code at the end of this chapter or visit the companion website and find Video 3.1 to hear Gracie explaining the product she created as a result of completing her grandmother's redesigned task.

Earlier we inspected the Cupcake Maker task for engaging qualities. That was before Terri "powered up" the task. Use the engaging qualities component of the Powerful Task Rubric in Figure 3.5 to inspect Terri's redesigned task.

1. Were there any changes in the inspection for engaging qualities?

FIGURE 3.5 Engaging Qualities Component of Task Rubric for Analysis

Engaging Qualities[**]	Personal Response (Clear/ Modeled Expectations)	Not necessary	Fill in the blank with "my" answer	Explain and support my ideas (open)	Explain and defend or justify my ideas
	Intellectual/ Emotional Safety	Not required	Not required	Expression of concepts or recognized patterns	Expression of supported opinions or new ideas
	Learning With Others	Take turns talking	Listen and repeat	Interdependence in roles or mini tasks	Interdependence of ideas
	Sense of Audience	A partner	The class	An audience I want to appreciate me or my ideas	An audience I want to influence
	Novelty and Variety	Recall is fun or different	Product without concepts	Product with concepts	Perspective
	Authenticity	Teacher connects to world	Repeat real examples	Recognize real examples	Create real examples

2. How did the knowledge and skills of the teacher/coach impact the redesign of the task?

3. Did the content change? If so, how did it change for the learner? How did it change for the teacher?

Before we move on, here is one final story of merit. The very tech-savvy Miss Montgomery, a 24-year veteran teacher from Indiana, shared her experience with technology and the importance of planning for engagement in her classroom:

> I have always felt it was important to plan engaging moments for my students. As a matter of fact, it's like a high for me, to see them excited and motivated about the content I want them to learn. However, I must admit, I have never given thought to the kind of interactions (visual, physical, social, cognitive) nor even if there would be a cognitive moment during their engaging experience.

Likely, there are others with experiences similar to Miss Montgomery's. As teachers, we are task designers who are only trying to be better tomorrow than we were today. A quality task designer does not look at engagement in isolation; rather, she looks at all components of the task (engaging qualities, strategies, and cognition), because together they make a more powerful design for learning. The authors of this book came together because we believe engagement is first about attracting attention and inducing participation. But engagement for the sake of engagement is simply fun. It is meaning that we seek. In the next two chapters, we will dig into strategies and cognition.

> A quality task designer does not look at engagement in isolation; rather, she looks at all components of the task (engaging qualities, strategies, and cognition), because together they make a more powerful design for learning.

To close this chapter, we invite you to apply what you have learned about the engaging qualities and the role of technology in your own content. If you are using the book as a book study or working through a professional learning community, ask its members to bring two tasks they currently have planned for their students. Facilitate an inspection, as a group, for engaging qualities. If you decide you would like to make the task more engaging, practice powering up the task by "slicing in" a particular engaging quality. You may find the Slicing in Engaging Qualities Tool (on the next page) helpful.

Slicing in Engaging Qualities With Digital Tools

Personal Response

How can I make multiple solutions possible? What can students bring to the activity from their own lives and experiences? What are possible digital tools that would make this process more efficient and effective for my students?

Considerations: image, poll, quiz, meme, video, podcast, website, discussion

Clear/Modeled Expectations

What do I want students to include in their answers? Are there examples/nonexamples I could find online? Are there tools to allow me to create my own?

Considerations: video, images, documents, drawings, screencasting software

Intellectual/Emotional Safety

How can I structure student talk to encourage different, less-obvious, or risky ideas? What digital tools are available to encourage students to participate in class by openly sharing their thoughts and ideas?

Considerations: Online discussion boards, back channels, online quizzes and forms

Learning With Others

What ideas will students compare or share? How will they explain, critique, or combine one another's ideas? What digital tool will allow my students to communicate and collaborate with one another? Are there tools that will allow me as their teacher to track, monitor, and provide feedback during their interactions?

Considerations: Cloud-based solutions with features for communication, collaboration, and feedback

Sense of Audience

Who (besides me and our class) would be a valued audience for this work? How would utilizing technologies extend the four walls of my classroom and provide authentic audiences for students to share their work?

Considerations: streaming video (live feed broadcasting out of the classroom), social media, blogs, web pages

Choice

What is another activity (or two) that would allow students to learn the same standard yet select between their activities? Are there digital tools to help me facilitate/manage offering multiple choices of assignments for my students?

Considerations: learning management systems, HyperDocs, QR codes

Novelty and Variety

What can we do to make this fun, goofy, or different (in procedure, product, perspective, or place)? What digital tools are available to help me present fun, goofy, or different products, perspectives, or places?

Considerations: photo editing tools, talking animations, videos, audio tracks, maps

Authenticity

What are the obvious real-world connections? Who does this in the real world? How could we simulate the real world in the classroom? How is this represented in the news? What online tools/services are available that would allow me to merge the real world with my classroom?

Considerations: virtual field trips, video conferencing with experts in the field, other students from other parts of the world

http://resources.corwin.com/powerfultask

CHAPTER 4

The Power of Academic Strategies

IT STARTS ON THE PLAYGROUND

When John was teaching kindergarten, he had an aha moment during the first week's recess duty. As he scanned the playground he realized that three of his boys were not to be found on the play equipment. He quickly spotted the boys on the back fence of the play yard—an off-limits area for the kindergartners. "Boys, come back to the playground now," John shouted. Young David looked up and yelled back, "No, you come over here!" John, the adult, returned the volley. "No, boys. You come over here!" David was persistent, "No, Mr. Antonetti, you come look at this. Come look at this!" David was pointed toward the grass at the fence line.

John went over to the fence. (The boys won!)

As he approached the boys, John realized they were watching a small black beetle walking in the grass. "What are you boys doing?"

Michael squealed, "Look at this bug, Mr. Antonetti!"

"Cool, boys. But we need to go back to the playground."

"Wait, Mr. Antonetti. Watch this." David leaned down toward the beetle and screamed loudly at the insect. The bug continued moving through the grass in a straight line.

"My turn," said Javon. And he screamed at the insect. The bug continued moving in a straight line.

"Now me," added Michael, who jumped in front of the beetle and let out another scream.

As the bug continued moving in a straight line, David summed up the playground analysis. "Did you see that, Mr. Antonetti? Bugs can't hear!"

"But watch this." David lifted his leg as high as he could and slammed his foot onto the ground just in front of the beetle and it immediately changed its course. As Javon and Michael began to stomp the ground around the bug, it kept changing directions.

David waved his arms to stop the boys from stomping and provided a final summary. "Did you see that, Mr. Antonetti? Bugs can't hear, but bugs can feel."

John recognized the value of the teaching moment. "That's right boys. Do you know why that is? On the segmented body of an animal we call an insect, the first segment—known as the head—has specialized structures that we call antennae. These antennae. . . ." And as John was explaining, the boys ran away, back to the playground.

> We are powerful and natural explorers.
>
> —John Medina (2008, p. 261)

As John stood on the back fence alone, he realized that the boys had just experienced the real learning and did not want to stick around for the PowerPoint slides!

It is this moment of discovery and curiosity that provides the most powerful learning—when students, working alone or together, can manipulate their surroundings to make sense of the world. It can happen in the real world of the playground or in the virtual world. It can be authentic or it can be simulated by technology.

In the Powerful Task Rubric, we believe curiosity is found in the visualized thinking strategies. We can even find an exemplar of one of the strategies in the now famous "Bug in the Grass Experiment of 1991."

Let's look at where we place this task on the rubric (Figure 4.1).

STRATEGIES OF PERSONAL RESPONSE

You may have noticed that academic strategies in the Task Rubric look different when compared to engaging qualities and cognitive demand. The latter two components exist in four levels, while strategies is divided only into three. This is due to the nature of teaching and personal response. We may design a task that does not require—or even merit—personal response. This would be a Level 1 task for strategy. We may design learning tasks in which the strategy is scaffolded or needs to remain under the control of the teacher. These are Level 2 tasks. But ultimately, students must take control of the strategy to make meaning in a task. Once the learner takes control of the strategy and uses it for cognitive engagement, the strategy becomes the vehicle for the personal response. Now the strategy crosses the rigor divide. We shall simply call it a Level 3 Strategy. The learner may *explain and support* her ideas *or explain, defend or justify* his ideas. There is a distinction in the extent of personal response, but both require ownership of the strategy. In other words, the power of strategy—and its relationship to rigor—is that it is mine as a learner.

FIGURE 4.1 Task Rubric: Academic Strategies and Engaging Qualities for *Bug in the Grass*

Academic Strategies*	Similarities and Differences	List facts about A and B	Parallel facts about A and B		Compare or contrast by trait
	Summarizing/Note-taking	Copy	Restate		Personalize or make unique decisions about content
	Nonlinguistic Representation	Copy other given forms	Place into other forms		Create a new representation
	Generating/Testing Hypotheses	Copy	Restate "known" pattern	Identify and extend patterns *(circled)*	
Engaging Qualities**	Personal Response (Clear/Modeled Expectations)	Not necessary	Fill in the blank with "my" answer	Explain and support my ideas (open) *(circled)*	Explain and defend or justify my ideas
	Intellectual/Emotional Safety	Not required	Not required	Expression of concepts or recognized patterns *(circled)*	Expression of supported opinions or new ideas
	Learning With Others	Take turns talking	Listen and repeat	Interdependence in roles or mini tasks	Interdependence of ideas
	Sense of Audience	A partner	The class	An audience I want to appreciate me or my ideas	An audience I want to influence
	Novelty and Variety	Recall is fun or different	Product without concepts	Product with concepts	Perspective
	Authenticity	Teacher connects to world	Repeat real examples	Recognize real examples *(circled)*	Create real examples

IDENTIFYING SIMILARITIES AND DIFFERENCES

As an instructional strategy, identifying Similarities and Differences includes various tasks that help learners see patterns and make connections. This is possible through one of four strategies: comparing and contrasting, classifying and organizing, creating metaphors and similes, and creating analogies. In *Classroom Instruction That Works* (Marzano, Pickering, & Pollock, 2008), the research shows the most intense effect size (45 percentile points) for a teaching strategy is identifying Similarities and Differences.

In a classroom visit to an elementary school in Kentucky, we find a fifth-grade teacher, Mrs. Duvall, introducing a social studies lesson on the American Revolution. She has her students in groups of three, and each group has one Chromebook. She has created a collaborative Google Sheet and shared it with her students. The purpose of the document is to capture the collective thinking of her students as they explore similarities between a hot topic for her young learners and the history content she must teach: *The Hunger Games* and the Revolutionary War.

Mrs. Duvall begins, "Boys and girls, I am wondering what you might know about *The Hunger Games*." Suddenly, hands fly up all around the room, and Carol says, "The last *Hunger Games* book has almost 500 pages, and I read every single word of it!!" Ty shouts out, "I have seen all four of the movies." The teacher is delighted to see the enthusiastic responses from her students. She continues, "Think back to our discussions about how good readers draw on their background knowledge to help them better understand what they are reading. They make connections to things they already know. It seems to me you have background information about *The Hunger Games* and we are going to use it, to learn about something new, the Revolutionary War. I think we will be able to make connections between the two events."

Mrs. Duvall explains the task:

> I have created a matrix using a Google Sheet to capture our thinking. Each group will be recording on the same sheet, so remember to be thoughtful collaborators and respect each other's space. When you pull up your sheet, be sure to change the color of your font to a unique color to represent your group. I would like each group to discuss possible connections between the two events. This could be connections between people, places, or specific happenings that occurred. Then record your thoughts/connections to our Google Sheet, and be sure to include the logic, reasoning, or explanation of how or why the two things are similar and provide evidence (link, image, etc.) to support your response in the appropriate boxes.

As the students begin working on their task Ty is overheard telling his other two group members, Jordan and Noah, that he is an expert on *The Hunger Games,* so he will be in charge of researching information about it. Jordan agrees and says she will be in charge of recording the information into the Google Sheet. Noah admits quickly he knows very little about the American Revolution but is happy to dig into the Explore feature in Google Docs and learn about it. He says, "If the American Revolution is anything like *The Hunger Games,* it is worth the work to learn about it!"

Mrs. Duvall allows students a class period to get started in their comparison. She reminds students that the important work of identifying Similarities and Differences is in naming the patterns they use to compare and contrast—just recording facts in the correct location of the graphic organizer does not "explain" their personal response. She also explains to them that today's work is an opening task and that they will revisit it in the upcoming days, and she provides some direct instruction on the Revolution. "Your work will actually inform us and tell us what we need to learn more about." But for now, the students are in control and they run with it!

A representation of the Google Sheet where they collaborated can be found by following the QR code at the end of this chapter, or going onto the companion website.

Let's take a look at this task on the Powerful Task Rubric under the component of engaging qualities (Figure 4.2). The students are asked to fill in an empty box, and also are expected to *explain and support* the connection as described in Level 3 Personal Response. Also, since the teacher requires that each response is supported with an explanation of how or why their answer is plausible, there must be a freedom to take risks in Mrs. Duvall's classroom, which indicates Intellectual and Emotional Safety. The students in this classroom are discussing possible connections between two events within their smaller groups. We know Ty's group has *assigned roles to perform mini tasks* among themselves to complete the bigger task assigned by the teacher; therefore this is Learning With Others at a minimum of a Level 3. When we look at the use of the academic strategy, Similarities and Differences, Mrs. Duvall has set the stage for her students to be using a Level 3 strategy by creating an assignment *comparing by attribute*.

SUMMARIZING AND NOTE-MAKING

Summarizing and Note-Making are both effective strategies to help students process information. When used effectively, these strategies have the power to capture each student's thought processes from inception to fruition. Personal Response should be the driver in a Summarization task, and at the very heart of every summary students write should be an opportunity to *explain and justify* their thoughts about their interaction with new information.

Personal Response should be the driver in a Summarization task, and at the very heart of every summary students write should be an opportunity to explain and justify their thoughts about their interaction with new information.

FIGURE 4.2 Task Rubric: Academic Strategies and Engaging Qualities for *Hunger Games*

Academic Strategies*	Similarities and Differences	List facts about A and B	Parallel facts about A and B	Compare or contrast by trait	
	Summarizing/Note-taking	Copy	Restate	Personalize or make unique decisions about content	
	Nonlinguistic Representation	Copy other given forms	Place into other forms	Create a new representation	
	Generating/Testing Hypotheses	Copy	Restate "known" pattern	Identify and extend patterns	
Engaging Qualities**	Personal Response (Clear/Modeled Expectations)	Not necessary	Fill in the blank with "my" answer	Explain and support my ideas (open)	Explain and defend or justify my ideas
	Intellectual/Emotional Safety	Not required	Not required	Expression of concepts or recognized patterns	Expression of supported opinions or new ideas
	Learning With Others	Take turns talking	Listen and repeat	Interdependence in roles or mini tasks	Interdependence of ideas
	Sense of Audience	A partner	The class	An audience I want to appreciate me or my ideas	An audience I want to influence
	Novelty and Variety	Recall is fun or different	Product without concepts	Product with concepts	Perspective
	Authenticity	Teacher connects to world	Repeat real examples	Recognize real examples	Create real examples
	Questions	Closed with single right or wrong answers	Closed but with a "choice" of answers	Open with a range of answers, support, strategies, connections	

Consider this example from a fourth-grade classroom. Mrs. Kimberlee wants to engage and empower her students to become active learners. Even during times when it is necessary for her to deliver information to students and expand their knowledge or broaden their perspective through lecture, she knows the students must be interacting with her in some capacity if their new learning is going to stick. She has noticed over the past few years one of the challenges her fourth-graders struggle with is the concept of summarizing. Some of her students write down everything she presents word-for-word, while others write down almost nothing. What she wants them to be able to do is to pull out the main ideas, the important details, the gist of the text.

She decides to use one of the most common forms of summarizing today—the #hashtag. Originally, hashtags were used in Twitter to categorize or group images, videos, and messages. This enabled users of the technology to search for specific hashtags and retrieve all relevant content in one search. In essence, if we choose to add a hashtag to a post, we should use it to determine the gist of the message. A guiding question to this thinking is, "What category(ies) best sum up the message?" It may sound simple, but determining the best keywords or the most powerful phrase to use to do the post justice is a difficult task.

Mrs. Kimberlee designed the task below. Give it a try!

Please follow the directions and complete the Summarizing task below.

Visit the companion website to find the photograph, video, and article referenced below. Your task is to

Create a one-word hashtag that captures the core meaning of the photograph.

Create a two-word hashtag that best represents the video.

Create a phrase hashtag that sums up the article.

Extra Challenge

Create a hashtag synopsis for the entire set with one or two words or a phrase.

Set:

Picture—http://barleyliterate.blogspot.com/2013/04/does-little-red-riding-hood-wear-camo.html

Video—https://www.youtube.com/watch?v=A8syQeFtBKc

Article—https://newsela.com/articles/lgbt-history-classrooms/id/19756/

FIGURE 4.3 Task Rubric: Academic Strategies and Engaging Qualities for Hashtags

Academic Strategies*	Similarities and Differences	List facts about A and B	Parallel facts about A and B	Compare or contrast by trait	
	Summarizing/Note-taking	Copy	Restate	Personalize or make unique decisions about content	
	Nonlinguistic Representation	Copy other given forms	Place into other forms	Create a new representation	
	Generating/Testing Hypotheses	Copy	Restate "known" pattern	Identify and extend patterns	
Engaging Qualities*	Personal Response (Clear/Modeled Expectations)	Not necessary	Fill in the blank with "my" answer	Explain and support my ideas (open)	Explain and defend or justify my ideas
	Intellectual/Emotional Safety	Not required	Not required	Expression of concepts or recognized patterns	Expression of supported opinions or new ideas
	Learning With Others	Take turns talking	Listen and repeat	Interdependence in roles or mini tasks	Interdependence of ideas
	Sense of Audience	A partner	The class	An audience I want to appreciate me or my ideas	An audience I want to influence
	Novelty and Variety	Recall is fun or different	Product without concepts	Product with concepts	Perspective
	Authenticity	Teacher connects to world	Repeat real examples	Recognize real examples	Create real examples

82

An analysis of this task is shown on the Powerful Task Rubric in Figure 4.3. A hashtag that sums up a message for a thought-provoking photograph or a suspenseful video clip should cross the rigor divide under the Power Component of Personal Response. In current reality, most hashtags we read on a daily basis on Twitter, Facebook, and Instagram have a Personal Response at a Level 2, as the writers just *fill in the blank with "my" answer*, which at most has signified a restatement of what has already been said. Sense of Audience is often at the root of why we hashtag. We want *an audience to appreciate our ideas*. Also, there is evidence of Novelty and Variety crossing the rigor divide as well. A well-done hashtag allows us to see a *product with a concept* that possibly enlightens us on a different perspective. As we look at this task to analyze the academic strategies Power Component Summarizing, writing hashtags, in the context of this assignment, should cross the rigor divide to a Level 3 by *personalizing or making unique decisions* about the content.

To clarify, the word *summarizing* is often used to describe the skill of paraphrasing someone else's thought or the act of simply recording a "briefer" version of someone else's thoughts. This version of summarizing does not cross the rigor divide. The power in the academic strategy is that the learner has a made a *unique decision about content*. For example, we might ask students to read and then summarize Chapter 6 in the Steinbeck novella, *Of Mice and Men*. Rather than asking students to retell the story or capture the important plot points of the chapter, we can add a more purposeful Personal Response question: "Do you think George is altruistic or selfish in his final action with Lennie? Use text evidence to support your answer." This type of summarizing requires the student to make a personal decision as a reader and to gather appropriate evidence from the text as a thinker and writer. Students will still have to understand the plot of the chapter, but they will not need to retell each and every event. The text-dependent nature of the summary requires them to selectively gather both explicit and implicit evidence from the text to support the Personal Response.

Figure 4.4 provides a ready set of template questions and reading/writing prompts to move the academic strategy of Summarizing and the engaging quality of Personal Response across the rigor divide. The cognitive demand of these tasks is also across the divide. This figure refers to the Common Core standards, but it certainly can be applied to any reading/writing situation.

NOTE-TAKING BECOMES NOTE-MAKING

When we have conversations with middle school and high school teachers and students about the strategy they most often use in the classroom, inevitably Note-Taking is named. In a typical high school setting, Mr. Carter kicks off his new school year by establishing his classroom expectations for the year. He tells his students, "Each and every day, you will need to come to class prepared to take notes. I will display a slideshow on the screen, and your job will be to take notes."

Literary Text	Informational Text*
What is the moral of the story?	Ideas: Should we or should we not allow . . .?
	Encourage?
What is the theme of the story?	Legalize?
	Abolish?
What did (character) learn that we all learn?	
Is (character) (attribute)?	People: Is (character) (attribute)?
For example, Is the Grinch brave? Is Ann cruel or careless?	For example, Is Jackie Robinson courageous?
	What was (historical figure)'s greatest attribute?
Which character in the story is the (attribute)-est?	
For example, Who is the kindest person in the movie?	Variation: In *Long Walk to Freedom*, how did Mandela deal with personal oppression?
How does (character) change in the story?	
Would (character) make a good _____?	Movements, historical periods, scientific discoveries:
	Was (character) a positive or negative influence on (the nation, a people, the acceptance of an idea)?
For example, Would Sharon from FreckleJuice make a good friend? Who will be the more generous spouse, Darcy or Elizabeth?	

*When opinion/argument writing is based upon informational text, the text must be robust; that is, it must present quality ideas and a sufficient quantity of information to support multiple claims. Since most informational texts present a single focus on a topic, multiple stimuli might be necessary. The opinion/argument thinking might be more meaningful after two or three different treatments are synthesized. Numerous Common Core standards require students to compare/contrast or synthesize multiple stimuli.

Likely, Mr. Carter's most motivated students will write word-for-word from the display, while the rest of the class writes only what follows the teacher's explicit words, "Make sure to write this down because you will see this again on the test!" We know Mr. Carter's use of this research-based strategy is not what Marzano had in mind when he and colleagues wrote *Classroom Instruction That Works* (2008)!

There is a distinct difference between "Note-Taking" and "Note-Making." The Summarizing/Note-Making indicators in the Task Rubric at Levels 1 and 2 feature the verbs *copy* and *restate* and refer to the student practice of simply recording the thinking the teacher has done or restating what the teacher has already said. Learners are accepting someone else's thought and not having their own cognitive moments. This process is Note-Taking, a teacher-centered task. As we cross the rigor divide and look at Level 3, we see a transformation in who is doing the thinking. Learners are personalizing and making unique decisions about how the content makes the most sense to them. This process is Note-Making, a student-centered task.

What might this look like in the classroom? Let's look at an example that comes from Sarah Landis (@sarahlandis), one of the three teachers who coined the term *HyperDoc* to define digital lessons. In the example below, Ms. Landis has created a HyperDoc to provide structure for her young learners to become note-makers. She sets a clear purpose for reading an online article to help her learners be able to answer the question, "Why do leaves change colors?" She explains to her students,

Boys and girls, while you are reading the article, if you come to an image or an important word or phrase that you think might help answer our question, I encourage you to capture it and place it on the left side of your note-taking page. When we take the author's thoughts and copy them onto our paper, we are note-taking. However, the most important part of this process is the right side of the page, because this is where you will be doing your note-making. This space is for your thoughts about how or why the image, word, or phrase taken from the author's work helps make sense of our purpose for reading, and that is to answer the question, "Why do leaves change color?"

We have had many conversations with teachers who tell us their students are much better readers offline than online. This news doesn't come to us as surprising at all. Good readers often leave traces of their thinking as they move through a piece of text. This procedure could take place in the form of sticky notes, highlighted sections, or notes in the margin as readers capture their questions, make inferences and predictions, and generate their thoughts! What we have just described is the real truth behind what makes a good reader—that the reader engages and interacts with the text. As powerful task designers, it is imperative we design tasks to scaffold the learning curve for our students as they transfer the skills they have learned to engage and interact with print text to a new context, one of a connected environment.

By choosing to design this task to be done online, Ms. Landis opens windows of learning opportunities for her students to engage and interact with the text. Her learners are now more likely to hone in on keywords or phrases and browse through hyperlinks, images, and perhaps even video clips to broaden their perspectives beyond the original printed text. Cognitive engagement with text—in print or online—is essential to developing a deep understanding of its content and ultimately to make sense of its meaning. Figures 4.5 and 4.6 show the HyperDoc Ms. Landis created and include two different ways that students interacted with it.

FIGURE 4.5 HyperDoc With Responses From a Student

Readers can develop a **deeper understanding** of text by jotting down **thinking** while reading an article online.

Click **HERE** for the article, *"A Change in Leaf Color"*

Don't forget that captions often have facts, too! Use this note-taking guide any way YOU want ... add a row, add images, etc.

When I read this part of the text ... (copy and paste words and phrases from ARTICLE)	... it made me think ... (copy and paste inferences from MY BRAIN)
chemical chlorophyll, gives leaves their green color, breaks down	Makes me think if something is breaking down it is not going to be the same as it was before it broke down.
other leaf pigments—yellow and orange—to become visible	This makes me think that others colors were always in the leaf too, but there must just have been more green than the other colors.
When days get shorter and cooler.....Leaves quickly lose their green color	I bet when it gets cold outside the leaves get cold and that is what changes their colors.

With your reading partner, **discuss** these questions:

HyperDocs created by @sarahlandis

FIGURE 4.6   HyperDoc With Responses From Another Student

Readers can develop a **deeper understanding** of text by jotting down **thinking** while reading an article online.

Click **HERE** for the article, *"A Change in Leaf Color"*

Don't forget that captions often have facts, too! Use this note-taking guide any way YOU want ... add a row, add images, etc.

When I read this part of the text ... (copy and paste words and phrases from ARTICLE)	... it made me think ... (copy and paste inferences from MY BRAIN)
When chlorophyll breaks down, yellow pigments in leaves become visible.	Chlorophyll is what gives leaves their green color so I wonder if when it breaks down it might be sort of like adding more water or other colors to paint, which creates new colors.
leaves change color when their food-making processes shut off.	This reminds me of what might happen if my food-making processes were shut off. I would change from a healthy pinkish color to a grayish dead color. So I am thinking when food-making processes shut off, it causes the leaf to begin a dying process and that's why it changes colors.

HyperDocs created by @sarahlandis

It is fairly common to hear teachers, particularly those at the secondary level, underestimate the importance of providing a required task of cognitive connection; they are proud to explain to us how engaged students are in their lectures and assume that learners are making cognitive connections of personal response. We don't doubt that this might be the truth, and have personally found lectures and TEDtalks to be powerful moments of learning, but we do have a follow-up question for any teacher who equates listening with learning. While the lecturer may hold the audience in a state of rapt attention, how do we know that the listeners are cognitively connecting? All that we can guarantee is that the learners appear to be listening and attentive. In reality, the students may be faking it.

> You can't be engaged in someone else's work; you can only be entertained by it.

The table in Figure 4.7 presents the interesting relationships—both causal and correlative—between thinking level and engagement as a factor of the engaging qualities of work. The percentages in the table represent the overall number of classrooms that were off task, on task, and engaged. They do not represent percentages of students within each classroom.

We recorded a classroom as "off task" when more than a single student would not commit to the assigned task or refused to work on the task. "On task" was recorded for the classroom task when almost all the of students were completing the assigned task. "Engaged" was recorded when all of the students were completing the assigned task *and* the task was designed with multiple engaging qualities.

For example, in classrooms where the thinking level required by the task was at the middle level of Bloom's taxonomy (a Level 3 in the Task Rubric), in 71% of the classrooms, the task did not include multiple engaging qualities. In similar cognitive tasks at the middle level, nearly one third of the classrooms featured full engagement in making meaning.

FIGURE 4.7 Cross Tabulation Between Engagement Level of a Classroom and Thinking Level

		Level of Engagement		
Thinking Level	# of visits	Off Task	On Task	Engaged
Low	14,898	4%	94%	2%
Middle	1,541	<1%	71%	29%
High	685	0%	58%	42%

Note: Data are from our Look 2 Learning study with a sample size of 17,124 classroom visits.

Based on the data in Figure 4.7, we see the thinking level of student work plays a critical role in the level of engagement. If kids are reading the text without a clear purpose or reason to want to read it, they likely will read it with the purpose of being compliant or on task. The big takeaway: Raising the thinking level increases engagement.

A common reality of practice across the country is the delivery of instruction through a combination of lecture and a slideshow presentation. Far too many times in this situation, the student task is to take notes by copying text from the screen. In this case, there is minimal interaction with the content. We have a couple of power-up recommendations for the lecturer. First, consider sharing the slides with your students either through an electronic link or a handout. Then change the task from asking your students to take notes to asking them to capture the meaning of the information presented (see Figure 4.8).

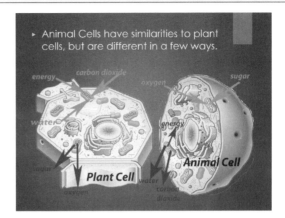

Teacher Created

Student Note-Making

Cell Structures
Both of cell types (plants and animals) also contain cell structures known as **organelles**

Shape
Animal cells have **round** or irregular shapes.
Plant cells are typically **rectangular or cube** shaped.

Cell Walls
Animal cells have **no cell wall** but **do** have a **cell membrane**.
Plant cells have a **cell wall** composed of cellulose **as well** as a **cell membrane**.

In the above example, the teacher shares the slide show with students before class and the students use the Notes section beneath the slide to make their own notes regarding both the slide and the lecture. Notice the student's notes reflect his thinking, and it appears he is comparing traits of cell structures.

Second, we encourage the teacher who lectures to purposefully plan to embed interactive, engaging chunks throughout the lecture to strengthen the learning experience for students. For example, by purposefully planning to pause the lecture from time to time and allow opportunities for the student to process the information and make sense of it can be an effective practice. In Figure 4.10 we see the breadcrumb trail of a student's thinking as he has labeled traits found in the cells (shape, cell walls) along with an explanation of how animal cells are similar to plant cells and how they are different.

Let's analyze the Note-Making task in Figure 4.8 using the Powerful Task Rubric. If we are students in this teacher's classroom, the expectation is the teacher will give us the notes he made about the "stuff" he wants us to learn. Our task is to *personalize or make unique decisions* about the content from our individual perspectives, by making notes. On the Powerful Task Rubric, we have crossed the rigor divide with the academic strategies of Note-Making and Similarities and Differences. As Figure 4.8 shows, during the note-making process, it is possible for students to use multiple academic strategies.

REFLECTION IN NOTE-MAKING

To make sense during Note-Making, students should make personal connections or decisions about content. Students can make meaning during Note-Making by using the other strategies in the chapter: identifying Similarities and Differences, Nonlinguistic Representations, and Generating and Testing Hypotheses. Yet many students do not know how to do so effectively and efficiently during the actual presentation of information or the recording of content.

Students can be shown a rather simple—yet effective—structure for reflective thinking known as the Four Rs of Reflective Thinking. First let's look at the definition of reflective thinking inspired by the work of Jennifer York-Barr (2001):

> Reflection: A present moment set aside to think about the past, so that we can look forward to the future.
>
> With this definition in mind, the Four Rs represent a structured approach to making students reflect on presented content. These are the Four Rs:
>
> Restate (present)
>
> React (present)
>
> Remember (past)
>
> Respond with questions or connections (future)

Find a 4Rs reflective worksheet available for download on the companion website.

For example, a high school English teacher, Mrs. Hampton, presents each of her students with a slide deck on propaganda in a version of a "flipped" assignment using Google Classroom. The students are expected to find a certain number of slides and make notes. The notes are to use the Four Rs structure. Figure 4.9 shows the notes that students added to the Google Slides.

Mrs. Hampton can see the notes as students take them in Google Classroom and can determine what information needs to be clarified or taken deeper. The students' questions from the fourth R provide the starting prompts for class discussion the following day. The Note-Making, then, becomes formative assessment that directs instruction to come.

Note-Making is rooted and grounded in Personal Response moments with the learner in control and making choices about the content during the processing of new information. It is impossible for Note-Making to have occurred if every student leaves the classroom with identical notes.

FIGURE 4.9   Student Notes Using Google Slides

Under Hitler's regime, propaganda was used to its fullest extent. Information available to the Germans was limited to that which cast the Nazis in a favorable glow. The idea was to eliminate opposition through a lack of information—documents that didn't uphold Nazi philosophies were burned. Meanwhile, radios were sold at dirt-cheap prices to allow everyone to hear Hitler speak. Films also facilitated the spread of Nazi goals; in these movies, Jews were compared to rats, Hitler was made out to be a godlike figure and Germans in other parts of the world were portrayed as being horribly abused.

Restate: The Nazis did all they could to make themselves look good and the Jews look bad. They used multiple media.

React: It's actually clever (and horrible at the same time) how they manipulated the media and people who probably were not evil.

Remember: I know how I "saw" people who lived in New York City from television and movies, but when I got a chance to travel with my mom to her office headquarters in New York, people were not what I thought. They were more like me than unlike me. They were friendly and polite and funny. One part was as expected. They did seem to walk everywhere or take subways or taxis.

Respond With Questions:
Who is using the media today? Corporations? Fossil fuel companies?
Is this the same as Fake News?
How do you know what is true?
Who's better at this? Liberals or Conservatives? Republicans or Democrats?

NONLINGUISTIC REPRESENTATIONS

The July 2015 edition of *TIME Magazine* includes an article by journalist Lev Grossman entitled, "The Old Answer to Humanity's Newest Problem: Data." In his story, he talks about the massive volume of data that humanity generates, going "from a world where information was hard to find to one where it's everywhere, in staggering quantities" (p. 42). He asks the reader to think about the use of the smartphone: "It's a communications device, yes, but it's also a tool for transmuting the world around you into data. You see something, you take a photo or video of it and upload it to the cloud, and it lives there forever" (p. 42). He goes on to say, "The best way to extract meaning from data is to make it visible" (p. 43).

When we take existing information in one form and represent it in a new form that demonstrates understanding, it is a Nonlinguistic Representation at a Level 2 on the Powerful Task Rubric. The power in this strategy comes when the task design includes opportunities for students to create their own representations and translations.

For example, in music class, the nonlinguistic translation is to *act* out the mood, the tone, or the rhythm (see Video 4.1 on the companion website). The teacher might ask the students to make a circle and move around the room to pantomime the staccato and precise rhythms of a Sousa march. When she changes the music to Tchaikovsky's Waltz of the Flowers, the students change their mood to match the new music. Finally, they take on a different set of physical traits when they hear Chopin's Sonata No. 2 (The Funeral March).

The translation is from auditory capture to kinesthetic representation. When the athletic coach shows the team the diagram in the playbook, and the team executes the play on the court, they have translated from one language to another—pictorial to kinesthetic. These are examples of Level 2 implementation of the strategy, as the learner creates a more personalized version of accepted knowledge. Nonlinguistic Representation crosses the rigor divide only when the learner creates a new version of the content to see the information in a way previously not understood. Even if we cannot guarantee rigor through a nonlinguistic task, we can assure better encoding of the content on the brain. Consider the following classroom example.

Mr. Bruce Ferrington, from Canberra, Australia, based a lesson with his students on the book *If the World Were a Village* by David J. Smith and S. Armstrong (2014). This book takes the world's population (which has numbers so large that kids find it difficult to understand) and imagines a world reduced to a village of 100 people. This is a more manageable number for students to understand, and it represents who we are, where we live, which languages we speak, the religions we practice, and more. After reading the book, the students in Mr. Ferrington's class created Nonlinguistic Representations in the form of infographics to translate the data into pictures. Check out the student work in Figure 4.10.

Infographics are a great way for kids to present information in the form of images with only a minimal amount of text, and they convey an easily understood synopsis of complex information visually. There are several

FIGURE 4.10 Student's Nonlinguistic Representation of Data

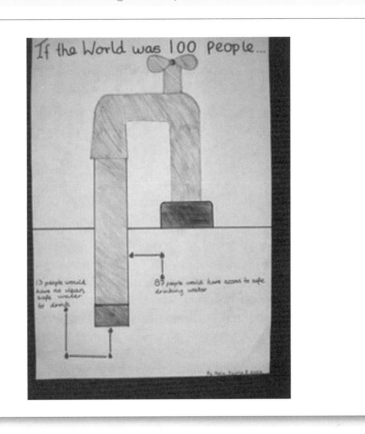

interactive, online tools that are specifically designed to create infographics. Piktochart (https://piktochart.com/tochart), Canva (https://www.canva.com/), and Venngage (https://venngage.com/) are three we see used most often in classrooms. However, as you can see from the student work in Figure 4.10, the students created their work by hand rather than generating it on a computer. We see creativity in both hand-created and technology-created forms of the student work; however, technology brings power to this task when the teacher showcases the work on his blog for the world to see.

Let's look a bit deeper at Mr. Ferrington's task on the Powerful Task Rubric. Under the engaging qualities component Personal Response, the task is at a Level 3, as

When a teacher makes a decision to post students' work to the web and the students know that there will be an opportunity to communicate with outside audiences who might truly *appreciate the learners' ideas,* there will be an increase in student engagement (engaging quality of Sense of Audience at Level 3). Perhaps even more compelling is the idea that sharing students' work on the web can have powerful connective experiences unimagined by the learners. The students who just had their information published in this book probably did not imagine it possible when Mr. Ferrington proposed the assignment. (Or did they?)

A caution about this strategy: If Mr. Ferrington had provided students a preconceived graphic organizer with a chart to fill out, we would consider it a Level 1 scaffolding of the strategy. Students might procedurally fill in the organizer—this goes here and this goes there, without ever seeing the relationships and the impact of the information. We do see lots of graphic organizers used in classroom tasks. Unfortunately, only 4% of the graphic organizers we've recorded in practice are student generated.

students *explained and supported their ideas* through graphics and words. As we stated above, the task has Sense of Audience. Novelty and Variety is present at a Level 3 with *products representing concepts*, and some likely made it to *perspective*. Each of the infographics represents a *real authentic example* as indicated in Level 3 of the Power Component Authenticity.

Now let's look at an example from Mrs. Wesley's mathematics class using the Nonlinguistic instructional strategy. Figure 4.11 shows the problem she presents.

FIGURE 4.11 Mrs. Wesley's Problem

Task

Explain the meaning of the following expressions and draw a picture that represents it.

$$(2 \times 4) + 6$$
$$2 \times (4 + 6)$$

How do you know?

Use Explain Everything to capture your thinking.

Watch videos of student explanations (Videos 4.2 and 4.3) by going to the companion website.

When we look at the student work samples, we see in Figure 4.11 the student's nonlinguistic representations are clear, accurate, and easy to understand. Observing the student work, Mrs. Wesley can see the student has made her thinking visible, and now Mrs. Wesley can see into the mind of the student and how she thinks about solving math problems such as the one provided in this example. The second student work sample, Figure 4.12, is a bit more challenging for the teacher to interpret. Obviously, there are misconceptions or inaccuracies in the student's scheme as it relates to order of operations. Adding technology to this task makes the student's thinking visible to the teacher. Now Mrs. Wesley not only can see the student's work but hear the student's reasoning in solving the problem. After watching and listening to the student explain her thinking, Mrs. Wesley can now provide effective feedback to address the student's thinking.

GENERATING AND TESTING HYPOTHESES

We often think of science when we hear the phrase *generating and testing hypotheses*. It does, after all, include the word *hypotheses*. That said, we will hypothesize in math and science first and then extend the strategy to language arts and the humanities. Ask any middle school science student what a hypothesis is, and the student will quickly say, "an educated guess." But, what is an educated guess? And what would an uneducated guess sound like?

If we as teachers recognize and remember that human beings innately and instinctively go to analysis when presented with new information, Generating and Testing a Hypothesis becomes the most natural strategy to fold into learning tasks. To generate a hypothesis, the learners need only be able to see something and make sense of what they are seeing. Analysis for the learner starts out uneducated—I didn't know what I was looking for until I saw it!

Since this is the most natural way young children learn, the strategy of Generating and Testing a Hypothesis should be easy to implement in the classroom; yet, it is dependent on three factors that are not always present:

1. Students must have the Intellectual/Emotional Safety to find, articulate, explain, and stand by their hypotheses.

2. Students must have their findings validated to ensure they are logical, reasonable, and rational.

3. Feedback should come through extension of the task or presentation of additional stimulus.

Teachers want to be efficient and effective. Unfortunately, efficient teaching can sometimes choke out effective learning. Put another way, we can tell our students something, or we can plan for them to find out. This struggle between teaching and learning starts with the design of a task, but is perhaps more difficult during the implementation of the task.

Let's look again at the three conditions for Generating and Testing Hypotheses and discuss the challenges of implementation.

1. Students must have the Intellectual/ Emotional Safety to find, articulate, explain, and stand by their hypotheses.

The biggest issue here is student conditioning to find the right answer. So many students will not propose an answer until they know what the teacher wants or will accept. This learned helplessness seems to increase as students get older and have experienced more school, more testing, and more failure, or even more success. One way around this debilitation is to ask learners to simply state what is true in the content, situation, or data. Asking students to tell a truth about what is in front of them may take away the need to be correct.

As an example, Mr. Hathaway shows his students an iconic photo taken at the Yalta Conference in 1945. He tells his students that the picture is a visual symbol that represents the involvement of the United States in World War II. Hathaway then asks his students to propose (hypothesize) what the picture symbolizes. After the students articulate a number of "guesses," the teacher says, "Tell me something true about the placement of the three men." Alicia says, "Churchill's on the left, Stalin's on the right, and Roosevelt is in the middle." Hathaway asks the class to consider what Alicia has said and then propose additional hypotheses. Joey immediately jumps in with "Churchill and Stalin were fighting and losing the war until the United States came in in the middle." When Trey's true statement is "the most important men are seated," Brady adds, "Roosevelt was crippled, so they would not want a picture of him in his wheelchair—that might look like weakness." Interrupting the hypothesizing to make sure we find the truths first adds Intellectual/ Emotional Safety and allows students to take risk of Generating the Hypothesis.

2. Students must have their findings validated to ensure they are logical, reasonable, and rational.

This is sometimes very difficult for us as teachers, since we already know what we wanted them to find. When John was first teaching kindergarten, his students were studying birds. When he was about to introduce a unit on penguins, he asked a question of his learners as they sat on the carpet: "We've been studying birds and generating traits about birds. Today we are going to look at some birds that don't fit the pattern. Some birds cannot fly. Who can think of a bird that cannot fly?"

Across the carpet, hands went up, but from the back of the carpet, Bubba (short for William) shouted, "I know one! I know one!" Although Bubba was not following classroom protocol, John was excited that Bubba was energized enough to respond.

"Bubba, what is a bird that cannot fly?'

All eyes turned to Bubba as he replied, "Um, um, a dead one!"

While the answer was not what John had hoped for, it certainly is a logical, rational answer. For Bubba's sake, John could only validate, "Boys and girls, is that true? Good job, Bubba, that is so very true. [Pause] Now let's think about a new question. Bubba, can you think of a living bird that cannot fly?"

"You mean, like a penguin?"

Yes. We have arrived.

3. Feedback should come through extension of the task or presentation of additional stimulus.

When we enter the testing phase of this strategy, feedback of "correct" or "incorrect" does not move students in their thinking. The correct student may have just been lucky that his answer is what the teacher wanted, while the unlucky, incorrect student may have actually been more thoughtful, more cognitive, and more referential. Incorrect, then, can shut students down or cause them to question their ability to make sense and meaning.

Feedback should require learners to struggle with the accuracy of their original claim—to validate, revise, or release their thought in order to articulate a new thought. We must trust that our learners can make sense with the additional information. As an example, Mrs. Koelher is teaching her students about regular polygons and lines of symmetry. Students have two-dimensional paper shapes of regular polygons and are asked to identify how many lines of symmetry each figure has. As the students work in pairs to manipulate the paper, they must also draw pictures of each line of symmetry and fill in the chart in Figure 4.13.

They complete their Note-Making with Mrs. Koelher adding an additional assignment. "Write a true statement using these words and phrases: *number of sides, polygon, lines of symmetry*."

Prentiss and Lamar wrote, "Polygons have the same number of lines of symmetry as the number of sides they have."

After reading this, Mrs. Koelher does not tell them if they were right or wrong. She asks if they are sure that what they said is true. They are quite confident,

FIGURE 4.13 Chart for Lines of Symmetry Task

Polygon	equilateral triangle	square	hexagon			
# of sides	3	4	6			
# of lines of symmetry	3	4	6			

and they articulate how their truth can be seen in the three shapes. Mrs. Koelher now asks the boys to test their hypothesis by finding the lines of symmetry for the trapezoid and rhombus (Figure 4.14). She reminds them that her additional task does not mean that they were wrong or right, but that she wants them to test their hypothesis. After Prentiss and Lamar recognize that the trapezoid has a single line of symmetry and the rhombus has only two lines of symmetry, they must revise their hypothesis. They now write, "Regular polygons have the same number of lines of symmetry as the number of sides they have. If they don't have equal sides or angles, they don't follow the pattern."

FIGURE 4.14 A Trapezoid and a Rhombus

TRUST THE LEARNERS!

Name the Thinking! There is one more consideration to keep the task strategy rigorous: The teacher must make certain that students capture the naming of the patterns, truths, or attributes they find. This naming of the thinking in this strategy leads to concept attainment and vocabulary development.

Let's go back in time and look at the concept attainment model. Based upon the work of Jerome Bruner (Bruner, Goodnow, & Austin, 2009), concept attainment is an indirect instructional strategy of Generating and Testing Hypotheses. Teachers plan for the seeing and naming of a concept, but do not direct learners to see it or point out what they are seeing. Students are tasked with figuring out the common attributes of a group or category or content by comparing and contrasting examples and nonexamples.

A kindergarten classroom might have a collection to consider that includes a hermit crab, a roly-poly (isopod), and a worm. The nonexamples might include a rock, a drinking straw, and a crayon. As the students brainstorm a list of commonalities amongst members of the example group, they may hypothesize that the group is living things, things that can move, or things you find under rocks. All of these are plausible hypotheses and exhibit analysis of commonalities.

It is then the teacher's responsibility (and privilege) to be fully present and prepared enough to provide more examples and nonexamples to clarify the plausible hypotheses to the concept she needs to reach. Simply forcing the learners to consider that a ship is another nonexample allows them to eliminate the things that can move and things you find under a rock. To further the testing of the remaining hypothesis, as well as bring more richness to the concept at hand, the class is then tasked with coming up with more examples of living things as well as nonexamples.

It is interesting to note that the same collection of creatures can be presented in an upper-grade science class to elicit the concept of invertebrates. The inability to actually see the absence of a backbone may cause students to struggle more to figure out the missing attribute, especially when the nonexamples are presented. Obviously, the nonexample set would be quite different from the set used in our kindergarten example.

In essence, Generating/Testing Hypotheses is finding patterns of similarity and checking for consistency within the group. We have found in classrooms two very important design considerations in planning these tasks: The original pattern set should consist of exactly three examples before including more examples. And those examples should look as different as possible while still retaining the essential attribute or concept. This allows the learners to compare two members of the group for an initial finding and then check it against the third as a safety test before the idea is articulated. The gradual addition of more examples keeps the brain from being overwhelmed while still demanding testing and reconfirmation of the original hypothesis, or revision to include the new information.

In some models of concept attainment, each example is presented paired to a nonexample. As an example, consider the game we often play in teacher training: "What's up with Billy? We will provide examples of things Billy loves and things Billy hates. At the end of the game, you may test your hypothesis by telling us other things he loves."

Billy loves **school** but he hates **learning**.

Billy loves the **zoo** but he hates **animals**.

If we pause after two examples, most humans will start to find relationships across the sentence pair—as if the activity were an analogies test. If we provide an additional example, it may present confirmation, but it more likely may require a new thought.

Billy loves **eggs** but hates **breakfast.**

We have learned that the pairing of examples with simultaneous nonexamples actually distracts most learners from the similarities within the example set and confuses students as they instead focus on the relationship between the example and nonexample. If we instead presented a list of only examples, the hypothesis is more likely to be "visible." To continue with Billy, he likes:

school zoo eggs cabbage yellow soccer cartoons Billy

The learner can now ask, "What do all of these have in common?" Any logical answer is the generated hypothesis. Now we present nonexamples:

work animals breakfast corn brown golf movies Bob

Clearly, Billy loves . . . words with double letters. Did you find any other similarities in the member set?

In summary, we've found the best method is to introduce a minimum of three concept examples, have students generate and articulate their ideas, test nonexamples, and finally confirm or revise their thoughts.

Another important bonus to using this strategy is the concomitant vocabulary development. We could even say that all vocabulary is based upon concept attainment. Mammals have very specific attributes, different from those of amphibians. Democracies have very specific attributes different from those of theocracies. Sonnets have very specific attributes different from those of haiku. Okay, you get the point.

Let's take this out of science and move into the arts. In a humanities class, the larger standard for the unit is as follows. Please participate in this activity and record your thoughts as we work forward.

Standard F. A. 1.6.9

Students will be able to compare and contrast masterworks in each of the major art movements of Romanticism through modern art.

The focus of today's lesson is to identify the attributes of Impressionism and to use proper art vocabulary when comparing Impressionism to Realism. Mr. Landers presents the class with three masterworks of Impressionism:

Impression, Soleil Levant by Claude Monet, *Un Bar aux Folies-Bergère* by Édouard Manet, and *Two Sisters (On the Terrace)* by Pierre-Auguste Renoir (see Figures 4.15 through 4.17).

FIGURES 4.15 Impression, Soleil Levant by Claude Monet

FIGURE 4.16 Un Bar aux Folies-Bergère by Édouard Manet

FIGURE 4.17 Two Sisters (on the Terrace) by Pierre-Auguste Renoir

To introduce the task, Mr. Landers says,

> These three paintings are world-renowned masterworks of Impressionism. I could give you a definition of Impressionism or you could figure it out. Your table group has eight minutes to look at the three paintings and come up with as many commonalities as you can. Don't worry about vocabulary or what to call what you see, just describe it. Jot down at least three short phrases to capture what you notice.

Here are the notes captured by three groups of four students in Mr. Lander's classroom:

Group 1

> They don't look right—like a photograph.
>
> They are blurry.
>
> You can't tell where everything starts or ends.

Group 2

> They are paintings of real things.
>
> They don't look posed like selfies.
>
> You can see colors up close, but they blend when you are far away.
>
> There are light and shadows in each one.

Group 3

> You can see the brush strokes.
>
> They are not precise.
>
> The colors are muted and come from mostly one side of the color wheel.

Using a Google Docs sheet, the students worked as a class to create a master list of 15 traits in the first column of the sheet. The class was then asked to discuss the list and to clarify or challenge any claims posted until all students agreed that the list was true and that all the traits were visible in all three works.

Mr. Landers provided a link to a website that described the birth and the history of Impressionism and characterized the style and techniques associated with it. The students were asked to compare their claims to the traits as articulated on the website. They were asked to find the "art vocabulary" that matched their ideas and place the descriptors in the second column. Figure 4.18 shows a segment of the Google Docs class document.

Since the students were essentially just finding a list of similarities in three visual examples of Impressionism, the visual nature of the task allowed for almost no "wrong" answers. In terms of task design, Mr. Landers had to make sure he had three examples that were different enough to allow for the similarities to stand out. By not expecting correct vocabulary during the analysis of the three paintings, he increased the Intellectual/Emotional Safety of the task—if I can see it, I can say it.

Generating and Testing Hypotheses is known by many other names across various curricula. When learners employ the strategies in this list, they are typically generating a hypothesis and/or testing it:

> Infer
>
> Predict

FIGURE 4.18   Class Document Showing Traits of Impressionist Paintings

Your original thought of common trait	Art Institute vocabulary
Blurry	Implied line Lack of detail
Colors not mixed together	Juxtaposition of colors
Real thing, not made up or abstract	Captured moment in time
Light and shadows	Play of light
You can see brush strokes	Broad brush Loaded brush
Make you think	Evoke emotion and mood rather than depict
Look different close up/far away	Blend of complements
Colors are warm or cool, not much black	Limited range of spectrum color

Analyze

Estimate

Guess and check

Draw conclusions

Question

In reading, we often ask students to infer—to find "right there" evidence in a text to generalize or predict how the characters might interact in the future. While reading *Pride and Prejudice,* the student comes to Austin's description of Lydia: "She will, at sixteen, be the most determined flirt that ever made herself and her family ridiculous." The reader may then infer (predict) that Lydia will bring disgrace or shame to the Bennet family. Reading further into the text will either confirm the prediction or discredit it.

The discrediting of a claim should not be a negative, but an invitation to think anew, informed by the previous hypothesis. Such is the case with the potent strategy of "guess and check" in mathematics. Unfortunately, we have seen students use this strategy on their own in only six classroom tasks (out of 17,124 visits).

In an algebra classroom in Florida, students were given this problem:

> Dan played three games of marbles. In the first game, he lost half of his marbles. In the second game, he won four marbles. In the third game, he won the same number of marbles as he had at the end of the second game. He finished with 32 marbles. How many marbles did Dan start with?

Many of the students began to work the problem backwards—reversing the operations. A few students drew pictures, while others made a matrix of the three games. As we watched Danyelle consider the problem, she decided to begin with number and (in her words) run it through the three games (Figure 4.19).

FIGURE 4.19 First Guess and Check

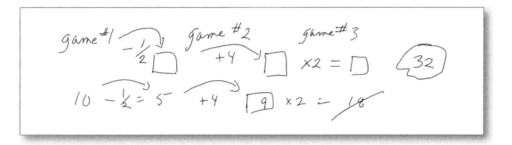

After determining that 10 would not work, she chose a second start of 15. When she got through the first game, she scratched out her work and started again with 20 (see Figure 4.20).

FIGURE 4.20 Second and Third Guess and Check

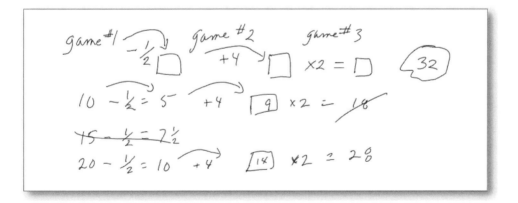

At this time, Ms. Merrill stopped at Danyelle's desk and asked her to explain the strategy. Danyelle shared that she was just trying to plug in numbers to get the right answer.

Ms. Merrill: Why did you start with that number?

Danyelle: I don't know, 10 just seemed like a place to start?

Ms. Merrill: So, what did you find out?

Danyelle: 10 wasn't large enough so I tried 15.

Ms. Merrill: Tell me why you didn't finish the line with 15.

Danyelle:	Well, at the end of the first game, he would have seven and a half marbles. I don't think a half a marble is possible.
Ms. Merrill:	What did you do next?
Danyelle:	I started with 20, but that wasn't enough either.
Ms. Merrill:	I see. Can you tell me something that is true about your guesses and your results? When you look here, do you see anything?

Ms. Merrill placed circles on Danyelle's paper (see Figures 4.21 and 4.22).

FIGURE 4.21   Teacher Feedback

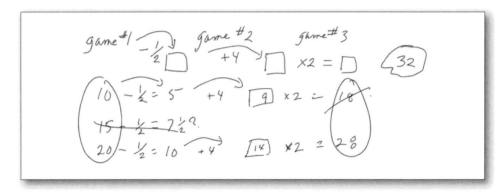

Danyelle:	Hmm. When my starting point went up by 10 (10 to 20), the result went up by 10.
Ms. Merrill:	(long pause and nod)
Danyelle:	So, if I need to end up with four more marbles, I should start with four more.

FIGURE 4.22   Fourth Guess and Check

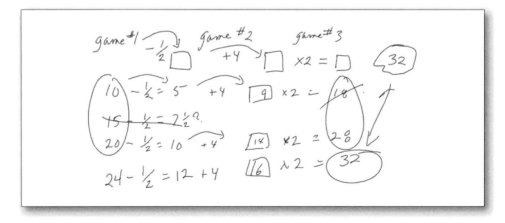

Ms. Merrill provided feedback in the process by asking Danyelle to not only continue the guess–and–check strategy but to articulate a found relationship in the problem.

REFLECTION AND CLOSURE

If Personal Response is the way we make sense of the our world, we must provide frequent exposure to tasks that allow student to make sense and meaning as they enter a task, rather than hoping for rich personal response at the completion of a task.

> Generating and Testing a Hypothesis may not be an educated guess as much as it is "educating your guessing."

Figure 4.23 illustrates how frequently, in our Look 2 Learning study, we encountered students completing tasks that required them to use the academic strategies listed in the Powerful Task Rubric at levels that took them across the rigor divide. The right column shows the percentage of tasks that moved across the rigor divide as the learner took control of the strategy and made meaning. Thus, another way to guarantee rigor is to design tasks that require the learner to take control of the strategies of meaning that have been discussed in this chapter.

FIGURE 4.23 Look 2 Learning Data

Strategy	Learner Control
Identifying Similarities and Differences	2%
Summarizing and Note-Making	4%
Nonlinguistic Representations	3%
Generating and Testing Hypotheses	1%

Sample size: 12,237 classroom visits

Respond to this data by generating two or three hypotheses about why this is reality in K–12 classrooms.

http://resources.corwin.com/powerfultask

CHAPTER 5

The Power of
the Question

To be or not to be. . . .

Wait, is that the question?

Read the two statements below and respond to one of them in writing. You may restate, react, remember, or respond with a question. Summarize or Note-Make across the rigor divide. Heck, you may do whatever you want—it's your personal response and your book. A five-paragraph essay is not necessary.

A task is only as powerful as the question underneath it.

A question is only powerful if answering it is not voluntary.

The next continuum we will consider is questioning. It was actually the last component piece added to the Task Rubric, but we chose to place it here in the book after engaging qualities and strategies of Personal Response but before cognition. We believe that questioning lands between engagement and thinking.

WHERE DOES A QUESTION COME FROM?

Conway High School in Horry County, South Carolina, offers a special teacher-cadet seminar class for high school students who think they might want a career in education. The students work in classrooms of many levels and learn the foundations of educational philosophy, history, theory, and pedagogy. A number of years ago, we had the chance to talk to students about their thoughts on good teaching. While we do know the grammar rule for prepositions at the end of a sentence, we still asked, "Where does a question come from?" The first three or four students who answered were clearly in school mode, not necessarily in learner mode.

"From knowing what you want students to learn."

"Sometimes from the essential question."

"From the curriculum."

It took a bit before Mariana asked us, "Did you mean when a teacher asks a question, or when the student asks a question?" We paused and—providing no clarification—asked again, "Where does a question come from?" Mariana stayed right with us and responded, "Well, either way it comes from needing to know something."

Any parent who has maneuvered a child through early developmental stages can tell you that questions come from—the three-year-old. Unending, unrelenting, and often even unanswered, questions become one of the most important cognitive milestones of a young child's development. *Why do dogs have tails? Why do they wag their tails? How come we don't have tails? Why? Why? Why?*

These questions usually come as a response to a stimulus—in this case, there is a dog, the child sees the dog, the mind gears up, and the need to know impels the questioning. Psychologist Michelle Marie Chouinard (2007) suggests that this form of questioning in young children comes from a place of "disequilibrium" as children recognize gaps in their knowledge or inconsistencies between the known and the new, or experience discomfort with the uncertainty in the present situation. The purpose of the child's questions, then, is to get the specific information that the brain wants or needs right now. This (sometimes desperate) *need to know* provides an especially fertile setting for deep processing.

While Chouinard is considering the role questions play in the cognitive development of preschoolers, we can consider her hypothesis as valid for all learners. If questions are a force in cognitive development, the following must be true:

(1) Children must actually ask questions that gather information.

(2) Children must receive informative answers to their questions if the questions are to be of use to cognitive development.

(3) Children must be motivated to get the information they request, rather than asking questions for other purposes such as attention.

(4)   The questions children ask must be relevant and of potential use to their cognitive development.

(5)   We must see evidence that children's questions help them in some way—that is, that they can ask questions for a purpose, and use the information they receive purposefully to successfully achieve some change of knowledge state. (Chouinard, 2007)

We think Chouinard has just described a learner in a state of wonder. This wonder—or natural curiosity—is essential to engaged learning. If we try to capture the natural learning process and incorporate it into a task design, we might simplify the sequence of curiosity to this: See-Think-Wonder.

SEE-THINK-WONDER

In a fifth-grade science classroom, Mrs. Jacobs presents her students with their first See-Think-Wonder task. We invite you to participate in her classroom and record your responses for the "Wonder Cycle" on the recording sheet (Figure 5.1).

See (Personal Response)

Mrs. Jacobs instructed the students,

> In a moment, I'm going to show you an interesting photograph. When you see it, you may be tempted to talk out loud, but I'm going to ask you to remain quiet for just a bit. Working by yourself, write down in your journal as many things as you can see when looking at the photo. Remember, do not jump to conclusions and do not think too much yet, just record what you see. When you share what you see, the rest of us should be able to see the same thing and should be able to point to where you saw it.

While the black-and-white photo presented in Figure 5.2 (see page 113) would suffice for our work, Mrs. Jacobs presented a more colorful—and perhaps more powerful—image that can be found on the companion website using the QR code at the end of this chapter.

Mrs. Jacobs adds a Learning With Others component to the task when she asks the students to work in pairs and take turns telling something they saw or noticed. "If your partner says something you did not originally see, point to what they said in the photo to make sure it is visible and that you can see it as well."

FIGURE 5.1 See-Think-Wonder Recording Sheet

What I SEE	What my partner SEES

What I THINK

What I WONDER

What I LEARNED

online resources ☞ Visit the companion website for a downloadable version of the See-Think-Wonder Recording Sheet.

As she walks around the room, the teacher hears Jasmine say to her partner, "It's a lobster." Mrs. Jacobs clarifies the task by reminding Jasmine of the present step. "It sounds like you've jumped to a thought, Jasmine, based on your *see*. Remember, in this step, we want to postpone conclusions or hypotheses. We are just saying what we see. What did you see that makes you think it's a lobster?"

Jasmine points as she responds, "It has a segmented tail like a lobster."

"Oh, yes. I can see the segmented tail. Let's record that and then hang on to the lobster idea for our next step in the wonder cycle."

FIGURE 5.2 Mantis Shrimp

Mrs. Jacobs checks in with the whole class, "How many of you saw something new after your partner shared?"

Think

Mrs. Jacobs next says,

> Now, it's think time. Write down the hypotheses, conclusions, or thoughts you have about what you see. You'll have three minutes. When you share your ideas with your partner, make sure you point to the part of the picture that gave you or triggered that idea. In other words, where is the visual evidence for your inference or the basis for your conclusion.

(We invite readers to commit their thoughts to paper.)

Wonder

Next Mrs. Jacobs introduces the third protocol,

> Now the most important part of our task: What do you wonder? What do you want to know about this creature? Make a list of questions in the box labelled "What I Wonder."

(Mrs. Jacobs is right that this is the most important part of the task. We invite the reader to commit your questions to writing on the reporting sheet.)

Students make a list of questions they have, including these:

What is this thing?

Is it related to a lobster?

Is it a shrimp?

Why is it so colorful?

Is this a male?

I wonder if it lives in the ocean.

Why are its eyes so high off its body?

Does it live in freshwater or saltwater?

What is it called?

How does it eat?

Can it swim or just crawl?

Can people eat it?

It is interesting to watch how students progress through the stages of See-Think-Wonder. One student might

> —see *it has a segmented tail,*
>
>> —think *it looks like a shrimp (since it has a segmented tail and lots of little legs)*
>>
>> —and wonder *is this a shrimp?*

This student's movement through the cycle may seem a bit shallow and perhaps like it is not much movement of thought at all. Nonetheless, he is making sense and moving toward meaning.

Another student might progress from

> —seeing *it has lots of bright colors,*
>
>> —to thinking *this could be a male (since males are usually more colorful)*
>>
>> —to wondering *how does it mate?*

This cycle shows a bit more evolution of cognition—from sight to curiosity.

A note to the timid: Some teachers might be uncomfortable with this last student's wondering about the mating habits and protocols of the creature. We find that many teachers are nervous about allowing students to self-direct the learning because it may go to ideas (or lead to research of ideas) that may be inappropriate for a particular grade level. When students take more control of their learning, the teacher must relinquish some control. This does not mean we lose control. Remember, we still determine the boundaries of the research process to come.

Find

Mrs. Jacobs asks students to share their questions with the whole class and then asks the students, "So how can we find the answers to these questions?"

The students immediately think of technology and develop a plan. The energy in the room is high. The unanswered questions are the disequilibrium, and the learners want to find the answers. "We can Google it!" As the students pull out their devices, it hits them. "Wait, what is this thing called?"

Mrs. Jacobs says, "I *will* answer *that* question for you. It's called a mantis shrimp."

"I knew it. I knew it was a shrimp."

"So, find out the answers to your questions and record what you learn."

The students have 10 minutes to conduct research. They begin to work independently, but in their excitement of discovery turn to share websites and information with each other.

(Again, the invitation. Please return to the reporting page.)

When the time is up, Mrs. Jacobs asks, "What is the most interesting thing you learned about the mantis shrimp?" Students popcorn around the room sharing facts and information. "It punches at the same speed as a .22 caliber gun." "It's eyes are the most complex of all animals."

A couple of students share the next questions they want to answer: "Can you eat it like other shrimp?" "Why have they been around for half a million years?"

Mrs. Jacobs shares a fact she found but does not tell the students exactly what it is: "The most interesting thing I learned is that I would never want to put one in an aquarium." When the children ask her why not, she simply responds, "You tell me. Maybe you can find out if I give you three more minutes."

Let's back up now and look at the See-Think-Wonder on the Task Rubric. The first step of the process is the collection of visual information—just look at the picture and describe what you see. Personal response is minimal, as the protocol is designed to limit students to a closed question with a choice of "right there" answers. *What do you see?* is a Level 2 question.

When we move into the Think and Wonder portions of the protocol, the thinking can move into Level 3 analysis as students Generate and Test Hypotheses: *it may be poisonous since colorful creatures like dart frogs and coral snakes are so colorful.* The cognitive opportunity of Level 3 in Think and Wonder typically gives way to a guaranteed Level 3 thinking as students

> become more familiar with the protocol,
>
> experience more interdependence with partners and their ideas,
>
> realize that they get to take more control of their learning, and
>
> do not have to be right in these steps.

When Intellectual/Emotional Safety and Learning With Others become the modus operandi in a classroom, this protocol crosses the rigor divide with great ease. The protocol becomes cyclical, in that students who find answers to their first questions may very quickly generate more questions. Our student who was interested in the mating habits may now ask—after learning about the female carrying the eggs—how does she eat and protect herself without hurting the eggs?

We have used the See-Think-Wonder protocol with adults during professional development and sometime struggle to stop the participants from digging deeper and deeper into the creature on the screen. As we move on to the next training component, teachers will continue to share what they are learning about the mantis shrimp. Curiosity and access to the connected learning environment are so powerful that we have to accept (and even celebrate) that we may have lost some control of the teaching.

> Unique and powerful ideas often are in the *questions* the learners asks.

In Chapter 2, we talked about an important filter question we must ask ourselves when we are analyzing tasks determining rigor: Are the students producing unique or new ideas? We may be conditioned to look for these moments of personal response in their answer to questions when, in fact, the unique and powerful ideas often are in the *questions* the learners asks.

WHERE DO TEACHER QUESTIONS COME FROM?

As seen in the task design above, when students ask questions, learning has a tendency to be more engaging and cognitive—more rigorous. Can we say this is true when teachers ask questions? Our classroom visits show us that teacher questioning is *all over the place*, or—perhaps—all over the continuum. And that is as it should be, since questioning can serve a wide range of purposes—from checking for accuracy to ascertaining concept attainment, from inviting all to participate to engaging deep cognition.

A number of years ago, we were asked to visit classrooms at Washington Middle School in Virginia (the name of the school has been changed for the purpose of this anecdote). We were walking with a principal who held a common definition of engagement: enthusiastic compliance. In our first classroom, we visited with two children while the lesson continued. Our student interview informed us that the task did not meet our standard of rigor in any of the four components from the left side of the Task Rubric—cognition, connection, strategy, or engaging qualities. But our conversation afterward in the hallway began with the principal saying, "Did you see that? She always has the kids engaged. Every hand was up." Our principal was looking at a behavior rather than the task at hand (pun intended).

To be fair, we should certainly celebrate that all of the children had their hands up. Student volunteerism and enthusiasm is both admirable and desirable in a classroom. As we continued through the building, we witnessed other classrooms where the energy was not evident and the volunteerism was minimal. As we left those classrooms, the principal registered his disappointment: "Not as much engagement in that class."

During our final classroom visit, we chose to interview a table group of students about their math task when the teacher posed a question to the whole class. We interrupted our interview so that the students could hear the question as she repeated it. We then paused to see if any of our interview group would volunteer. No one from our group spoke nor raised a hand. John prompted the small group, "Okay, who's going to answer?"

One young lady shared quietly, "I wasn't sure what she meant by the question," as a girl across the room proposed an answer that was validated by the teacher.

As we left the classroom, Terri wondered aloud, "What causes such a wide range of volunteerism between classrooms in this—or any—building? Or even between students sitting within the same classroom?"

At the time, our current version of the Task Rubric already included cognition, strategies, and engaging qualities. The visit to the Virginia school had become our own See-Think-Wonder. We wanted to learn more about the relationships between teacher questions and engagement and cognition. In a review of literature on the topic, we found a powerful, user-friendly connection in *Quality Questioning* by Jake Walsh and Beth Sattes (2005). We decided to incorporate their simple but elegant taxonomy to look at questions based upon the cognition they require of the learners: *recall*, *use*, and *create*.

According to Walsh and Sattes,

> Young children can easily distinguish between questions that ask them to (1) simply recall what they have learned, (2) do something with what they have learned, and (3) use their imaginations to go beyond what they have learned or been told.

Task Rubric Questions Take 1

Our first iteration of the question continuum looked like this (Figure 5.3).

FIGURE 5.3 First Iteration

Power Component	1	2	3	4
Questions	Recall		Use	Create

When we first decided to employ the Walsh-Sattes taxonomy during our visits, we found the taxonomy immediately effective as a tool. Yet, after coding and categorizing visits in three or four schools, we experienced what can only be called a BFO—blinding flash of the obvious! We were so busy recording the cognitive level, we were categorizing questions that were answered by a *single* student or a few volunteers. We were distracted from our original intent of looking at the task design and the thinking demanded of ALL learners.

Perhaps the data set in Figure 5.4 can illustrate our point.

In our 17,000 classroom visits, 49% of all of the classrooms involved a teacher-centric focus. In other words, students were listening or watching a teacher as the deliverer of information. While these numbers often surprise teachers, we must note that the data points in the chart below are neither positive nor negative; they only record the "control" of the work in the classrooms during the visits. Embedded in the "listening/watching" numbers is teacher questioning that did *not* become a required task for all students. When answering a question became compulsory for each learner in the class, it was considered a task and is reported in the third column.

We now only consider the cognitive demand of a question if it becomes a required task for all. Teachers often ask high-order, thought-provoking questions, but the resulting discussion might only involve five or six students, while another twenty-three listen to the discussion. For this reason—regardless of the cognitive expectation of the question—we record the cognitive

FIGURE 5.4 Primary Student Activity by Grade Cluster

Look 2 Learning Data

Primary Student Activity by Grade Cluster

Grade Levels	Activities Involving Listening/Watching	Task(s) Required of All Students*
All Classrooms (PreK–Grade 12)	49%	42%
Primary (PreK–Grade 2)	37%	56%
Intermediate(Grades 3–5)	43%	44%
Middle School (Grades 6–8)	52%	38%
High School (Grades 9–12)	63%	28%

Sample size: 17,124 classroom visits

*This reporting category includes all visits in which all student were involved in a task.

demand of the task at a Level 1. Again, there is no judgment here about classroom practice—only a recognition that we cannot gauge the level of cognition employed by the passive listeners. Indeed, we cannot even assure that there is cognition; at best, the demand for all students is a Level 1.

While we continued to struggle with whether or not questions belonged in the Task Rubric, John got a call from a large district in Texas that was planning to build a new alternative school. To best meet the needs of their at-risk population, the superintendent wanted John to interview at-risk students about what changes would make them want to come to school. The architects had been hired, but they were asked to postpone design proposals until we gathered and presented what students told us. John met with four different groups of at risk-students (as well as the National Honor Society officers, for some reason). All five groups repeated the same recommendations, which included using more technology, self-pacing, and interest-based and project-based learning. They asked for more collaboration and more hands-on and authentic work, with less lecture and teacher talk.

One of the at-risk groups took us into a surprising conversation centered around questioning. One of the students said, "Teachers should ask us questions and then let us talk."

Others chimed in. "Maybe *make* us talk."

"But only if the question is worth talking about."

A third student added, "and don't answer your own questions or get too excited when the hairbows answer." (Note: John learned that *hairbows* is a somewhat derogatory reference to the students who are good at school and like to get attention for doing what is expected.)

A final statement by a young man elaborated on a sentiment from the classroom visit mentioned earlier: "I'm not always sure what my teachers want when they ask a question. With Mrs. Nelson, I'll answer a question, and she'll be like 'Wow, Trevor, I never thought of that.' I like questions like that—when my answer can surprise her."

If the learners do not understand the purpose of our questions, we can't be surprised by varied responses to teacher questions. We are not talking students' answers here, mind you, but their emotional reactions and cognitive expectations. Our at-risk student focus group shared that these are the first thoughts they have when asked a question in class:

> Is she asking if I know the answer or trying to find out what I know?
>
> What does he want me to say?
>
> Am I supposed to know the answer?
>
> Are you asking for my personal thinking?
>
> Is this rhetorical?
>
> Who gets to answer this question?
>
> Who has to answer this question?
>
> Can I have a different answer?
>
> Are you going to tell us the answer if we don't get it?
>
> Can I argue/Will I get to explain my answer?

The students were not talking about cognition as much as they were describing engagement and—more specifically—the quality of Personal Response.

There are many reasons teachers ask questions—to check for understanding, to manage the classroom, to provide feedback, and to increase engagement and impact rigor. With this in mind, and to incorporate what our Texas students taught us, we wanted to focus on the "invitation" of Personal Response the question provides.

Michael Stevens, the persona behind the YouTube sensation Vsauce, regularly poses questions for his 5.5 million subscribers. Past questions have included those shown in Figure 5.5.

FIGURE 5.5 Vsauce Questions

What color is a mirror?	Why do we have two nostrils?
How much does a shadow weigh?	What makes something cute?
What if everyone on earth jumped at the same time?	What defines something as art?
What's the most dangerous place on earth?	

In a TedX talk that explores the success of his channel, Stevens provides some insight for all teachers and task designers:

> Why do we ask questions? To bring people in, to make them curious, and once they are there, accidentally teach them a whole bunch of stuff about the world.

A link to this TedX video is available on the companion website.

Task Rubric Questions, Take 2

Our second iteration of the question continuum is shown in Figure 5.6:

FIGURE 5.6 Second Iteration

	Power Component	1	2	3	4
	Questions	THE expected answer	My answer	My own thoughts	

This connection to engagement gave the tool a better focus on Personal Response—it was not the cognitive demand, but the student's reception of the question and ownership of the answers. At the same time, it captured and highlighted a familiar issue associated with school—do we value learning (Levels 2 and 3–4) or learnedness (Level 1)?

> As an extension of growth mindset research,
>   Do we value learning or learnedness?

In a frequently utilized kindergarten readiness assessment, young children are asked the question "Where do you live?" The administration manual states that if the child's response is "incomplete" (e.g., "I live with grandpa" or "I live in a house"), the adult should ask additional questions such as "Where is your house?" or "What is the name of your street?" This is the underlying "readiness" answer. The student only receives credit if she gives her street address.

If you read this testing scenario and think it unfair to the learner, you have come to the same realization we did about the role of questioning in a task. So now we moved to a third iteration: a continuum that represented what was required for an answer to be correct. We finally found in the work of Marian Small the structure for which we had been searching. In her book *Good Questions: Great Ways to Differentiate Mathematics Instruction in the Standards-Based Classroom* (2017), Small suggests that an "open" question—and the task required by it—can differentiate instruction and meet the needs of a variety of students simultaneously. She describes an open question as one that is "framed in such a way that a variety of responses or approaches are possible" (p. 7).

Question 1: To which fact family does the fact $3 \times 4 = 12$ belong?

Question 2: What mathematical equation can describe the picture below?

X	X	X	X
X	X	X	X
X	X	X	X

Small explains the difference in the two learning tasks in the box above in this way:

If the student does not know what a fact family is, there is no chance he or she will answer Question 1 correctly. In the case of Question 2, even if the student is not comfortable with multiplication, the question can be answered by using addition statements (e.g., $4 + 4 + 4 = 12$ or $4 + 8 = 12$). Other students might use multiplication statements (e.g., $3 \times 4 = 12$ or $4 \times 3 = 12$), division statements (e.g., $12 \div 3 = 4$), or even statements that combine operations (e.g., $3 \times 2 + 3 \times 2 = 12$). (Small, 2017, p. 7)

Since the idea of closed or open referred to the specified question and the design of the underlying task, we felt like we had arrived at a constructive vocabulary for the continuum. The words also captured the concerns of our students in Texas: Are we supposed to have a Personal Response (open) or just the right answer (closed)?

Consider the questions in Figure 5.7 from other content areas that move from closed to open:

FIGURE 5.7 Questions That Move From Closed to Open

Closed	*Open*
When was the Magna Carta signed?	Generally speaking, why do people sign documents? How does this apply to the historical context of the Magna Carta?
What is the subtitle of *Tess of the d'Urbervilles*?	What is a better subtitle for *Tess of the d'Urbervilles: A Pure Woman Faithfully Presented*? (Explain using evidence from the text.)
What is ½ of 240?	The answer is 120. What fraction of what number could it be?
How many legs does a spider have?	When you think about a spider, what might be the advantage of having the number of legs it has?

As we continued to look for the causal relation between student engagement and teacher questions, the continuum went through one more iteration after we visited Sarah Petit's third-grade classroom.

Mrs. Petit: We've read a number of fables this year. Who remembers what a fable is?

All hands go up. Tanya is invited to answer.

Tanya: A short story that teaches a moral. It usually has animals in it.

All hands go down. The rest of the class recognizes that this is a closed question and Tanya has successfully provided *the* correct answer. Done.

Mrs. Petit: Who can think of a fable we've read?

All hands go up. Barron is invited to answer.

Barron: *The Ant and the Grasshopper.*

Two hands go down, but the rest are still up.

Mrs. Petit: Good. Paula?
Paula: *The Tortoise and the Hare.*
Sam: *The Green Frogs.*
Layla: *The Greedy Dog.*

Because this question has more than a single possible answer, more students are able to participate. This became our "middle possibility" on the question continuum—*closed but with a "choice" of answers*. This is known as a content-centered choice.

Another version of a more participatory closed question results from a person-centered question. The range of accepted answers is broader simply because children have different backgrounds, experiences, or schema. The initial question in our kindergarten readiness screening actually starts at this middle entry point. The correct answers (from the children's point of view) can be numerous: "I live in an apartment," "I live down by the lake," "I live in Connecticut," "I live with my grandma." To each child, the answer is still closed and true, but different from my neighbor's answer. The question does not push the engaging qualities across the rigor divide, but could certainly be powered up with a follow-up of open questions and some pattern finding. "So, let's think about all the different answers we just heard. Can we put our answers into categories? What patterns did you hear? Which answers go together?"

Task Rubric Questions Take 3

Figure 5.8 shows our third iteration of the question continuum.

FIGURE 5.8 Third Iteration

Questions	Closed with single right or wrong answers	Closed but with a "choice" of answers	Open with a range of answers, support, strategies, connections

John Hattie (2012) places questioning in the domain of the teacher and reports an effect size of 0.48, clearly in the middle of influence on learning achievement. Could this average effect size be simply that—an average of the impact of all of the questions asked in school, regardless of their purpose, nature, or design? Our classroom visits suggest that a question can be opened to power up engagement, strategy, and—most important—cognition across the rigor divide.

HOW TO OPEN A QUESTION

There are a number of ways to take a closed question and open it for Personal Response. While we hope these protocols are helpful, we would ask you to be most mindful of how the opening (or powering up) of the question impacts the other components in the Task Rubric.

Question the answer.

Ask for a sentence of truth.

Identify similarities and/or differences.

Ask for a personal decision.

Change the language of response.

Ask for a hypothesis.

Change the question.

Question the Answer

Questioning the answer is a bit like the Jeopardy game show. Instead of asking a question, the teacher proposes an answer, and the students propose a question that is an appropriate match. Figure 5.9 gives some examples of closed questions turned into open questions by using this technique.

FIGURE 5.9 Examples of Questions Opened by Questioning the Answer

Closed	Open
What is the hypotenuse of a right triangle if the legs are 3 units and 4 units long, respectively?	One side of a right triangle is 5 units long. What could the other side lengths be?
Who wrote *On the Bus With Rosa Parks*?	The answer is Rita Dove. What might the question be?

In a seventh-grade English class, Ms. Mary Beth Alexander opened a unit on poetry by asking her students to consider the open Rita Dove question as a bell-ringer or a do-now introductory task. They were given five minutes and access to technology to come up with as many questions as they could.

Students responses included the following:

Who was the first African American poet to serve as Poet Laureate Consultant to the Library of Congress?

Who won the Pulitzer Prize for poetry in 1987?

Who wrote about her mother's parents in the poetry collection *Thomas and Beulah*?

What poet collaborated with John Williams on the orchestral song cycle *Seven for Luck*?

As they approach the five-minute mark, Alexander asks her students to decide which question provides the most insight into what kind of poetry we might expect to read by Rita Dove.

Ask for a Sentence of Truth

Students are given a series of words or numbers and asked to combine them into a true statement or claim. The engaging quality of Intellectual/Emotional Safety is present when students get to think in—and articulate—their own true statements. Rather than the teacher emphasizing the "rightness" of the response, other students can be asked to decide if the statement holds true. When it is *not* found to be true, the original thinker is asked to revise her thinking (or sometimes just her word choice or syntax). Figure 5.10 shows examples of this technique.

FIGURE 5.10 Examples of Questions Opened by Asking for Sentences of Truth

Closed	Open
What is the opening emotion presented in the first stanza of Wordsworth's *Daffodils*?	What true sentence can be written about *Daffodils* that includes the words *emotion, change,* and *stanza*?
What is the definition of political injustice?	What true sentence can be written using the following terms: *political injustice, primary wound, secondary wound*?
What are the seven oceans of the world?	What true sentence can be written that includes the names of two oceans and one land mass?
What is a linear pattern?	What true sentence can be written that includes the words *linear* and *increasing* and the numbers *4* and *9*?

The math students who answer this last question might produce a variety of sentences such as the following:

An *increasing linear* pattern could include the numbers *4* and *9*.

In a *linear* pattern starting at *4* and *increasing* by *9*, the tenth number will be 85.

A *linear* pattern that is *increasing* by *9* grows faster than one that is increasing by *4*. (Small, *More Good Questions*, 2010, p. 26)

It was this technique of opening a question that provided the anticipatory activity at the beginning of this chapter. In the end of a recent workshop on task design, we asked teachers to reflect on their learning by writing a true sentence with the words *question* and *powerful*. The statements presented on the first page of this chapter were two of the responses we received.

Change the Question

Often, we can take a question from a text series, assessment, or other resource and use it as a starting place. Figure 5.11 provides some examples.

FIGURE 5.11 Examples of Questions Opened by Changing the Question

Closed	Open
What is the cosine of angle C?	The cosine of an angle is a lot more than its sine. What do you know about the angle?
What was the meaning of the word *anticipatory* in the passage?	Why do you think the author chose the word *anticipatory* in the passage?
What is the cultural setting of the story *Erandi's Braids*?	How does the cultural context influence the Erandi character in the story *Erandi's Braids*?

Although the closed question about *Erandi's Braids* asks readers to think about culture, most readers think that the focus of learning is about this particular text. The open question moves the learners into a bigger expectation—we are learning about culture and how a writer's culture or the culture of a story impact meaning, mood, and tone.

The next four strategies for opening a question are literally just that: strategies of Personal Response from Chapter 4.

Identify Similarities and Differences

As a reminder, the secret to rigor in this strategy is that the learners should be naming the attributes or traits by which they compare and contrast, rather than just articulating things that are true about both or true about one but not the other. Figure 5.12 provides examples.

At the beginning of a professional training on rigor and strategies, we asked a version of the final question in Figure 5.12. The first teachers in the workshop to share compared district training days to

Cheerios   They can both be good for you, but they are often bland.

Nike   Both will take you far if you "just do it!"

Cialis   (We choose not share this one. You are free to come up with your own similarities and differences here.)

Closed	Open
How does Jem describe Boo in Chapter 1?	Which other character in the novel is most like Boo Radley? Explain your answer.
Which of the following fractions is a number less than one? $\frac{5}{8}$ or $\frac{8}{5}$	How are the fractions $\frac{5}{8}$ or $\frac{8}{5}$ similar and different?
What is our current professional development goal?	Consider a product you see advertised on television. How is that product similar to professional development?

Summarizing and Note-Making

This opening of a question requires students to make a decision about content as their answer—or as part of their answer (Figure 5.13).

Closed	Open
What are the factors of the polynomial shown here? $x^2 - y^2$	Which of the following polynomials is the most difficult to factor? Why? $x^2 - y^2$ $ax^2 + bx + c$ $x^2 + bx + c$ $x^3 + y^3$
Unhei chose not to share her name with her class. How does the class react?	Do you think that the class cares which name Unhei chooses? Will it make a difference? Why or why not?
What are three of the programs enacted under the New Deal?	Which three of the New Deal programs have had the longest lasting positive impact on the citizenry of the United States?

Students were arranged in groups of four for the final question in this set. They were asked to come to consensus regarding their answers, if they could. As individuals began to explain their personal response, it became clear to the groups that they were all interpreting the question differently. They began to argue which part of the question was the most important: *longest lasting*, *positive* (according to whom?), and citizenry (during the time of the New Deal or our current welfare state?). The nebulous wording and the confusion about the question actually enhanced the openness of question—for the learners could all argue why each of their disparate answers was correct.

Nonlinguistic Representation

As the question is opened in this strategy (Figure 5.14), the learners are forced to answer in a different modality than that used for the presentation of content material.

FIGURE 5.14 Examples of Questions Opened Using Nonlinguistic Representation

Closed	Open
What is Manifest Destiny?	How could you draw a single picture that captures the nine ideas we discussed about Manifest Destiny?
What is the name of the technique used in Stanza 8, "... that flies fearless and fleet"?	What music should be playing behind this stanza to capture the mood? How does the author's word choice inform your decision?
How do you simplify $5(2x + y)$?	What drawing from your real world captures the idea represented in the expression $5(2x + y)$?
At Measure 118, what does the marking *animato* mean? At Measure 167, what does the marking *con brio* mean?	How would you have an *animato* conversation with a friend? Act it out. How would you transition the conversation *con brio*? Show me.

As Mr. Gregory presents a new piece of music to the band for sight reading, he directs the students to the measures that transition mood, style, and articulation. He asks the students to imagine that they are in conversation with a friend, and he wants them to act out the changes across the piece before they play them. This increases the likelihood that musical expression will be a part of their first run through (as well as—he hopes—correct notes and rhythms).

Generating and Testing Hypotheses

To open a question in this strategy (Figure 5.15), we must ask the learner to think forward.

In an Advanced Placement psychology class at Mundelein High School near Chicago, Mrs. Schaefer is introducing group dynamics theory. She

FIGURE 5.15 Examples of Questions Changed by Asking for a Hypothesis

Closed	Open
In Chapter 4 of *Lord of the Flies*, how do Jack and Piggy interact?	Of the interactions between Jack and Piggy or those between Jack and Ralph, which do you think are most likely to move the rising action in the chapters to come? Why?
How many fruit-flavored candies should I buy if I want each of our 27 classmates to have 5 candies?	I want to buy everybody in our class 5 fruit-flavored candies. Without "doing the math," what is a number of candies that would not be enough? What is a number of candies that would be too many? How do you know?
What is meant by conformity?	Look at the three pictures presented here. If they capture an idea about group dynamics, how would you finish this generalization: "When people are in groups, they_____."

has three pictures on the SmartBoard. The students are presented with the final question in Figure 5.15 and share their responses in a Google Classroom Document. The teacher has toggled off the selection for students to view others' input, so they cannot see each other's answers. Mrs. Schaefer waits until all students have responded (thus guaranteeing each student's own Personal Response before other classmates lead them into simply repeating ideas posted and shared) and then reveals the class thinking. Based upon the pictures, the student responses include the following:

When people are in groups they want to be like everybody else.

When people are in groups they want to fit in.

When people are in groups they don't want to be different.

When people are in groups they start to act the same.

Mrs. Schaefer reviews a variety of responses, asking if the rest of the class can also see what their classmates saw in the picture. Finally, she asks the students to propose a name for the phenomenon they are witnessing. *Peer pressure, obedience, conformity, acceptance.* Schaefer's students are primed—actually eager—to hear the accepted answer. When she announces that they are looking at examples of conformity, some students actually cheer. She then shares Solomon Asch's Swarthmore studies (1951) and his theories of group dynamics.

TECHNOLOGY AND QUESTIONS

Technology allows teachers to make sure that all students are participating in answering questions. Depending on the question's task, this can also increase Personal Response to include all learners. Over the past few years, we have observed this inclusive practice through the use of student response systems (also called clickers). These systems can be hardware with software packages, TV game show–like templates, or web-based solutions. For example, Socrative, Soapbox, Poll Everywhere, Kahoot, Today's Meet, Google Forms, Go Formative, and Quizziz are all web-based response tools that allow students to key in responses (using a mobile device) to questions and immediately receive feedback. The efficiency, transparency, and immediacy of generating timely student data and providing appropriate feedback has the power to transform teaching and learning in remarkable ways. However, more times than not, we see these tools used to assess what students have already learned through closed, factual, and knowledge-level questions. While these experiences may be fun and have many engaging qualities, to know the potential impact on learning, let's look at an example through the Powerful Task Rubric.

Mr. DeVore has his students working in pairs. Trey is facing the screen where he sees a TV template. Sophie Grace has her back to the screen. She attempts to guess a series of science vocabulary words, phrases, or important names and dates based on descriptions given to her by Trey. The selected words or phrases come from the content the class has been learning about over the past two weeks. Theoretically, Trey would need to be able to *explain their ideas* as they relate to the science content, and Sophie Grace would *understand* the science content at a level to respond to the description by *filling in the blank with the answer*. The game style approach has many engaging qualities, but what kind of thinking is required for students to be successful in the game? It is likely that the students will be successful on the vocabulary they already knew prior to the game. If the students do not know the facts and vocabulary at an automatic level, it is also likely that the game—while fun and novel—will not "teach" the content the students do not already know.

Let's go into a different classroom, where Mrs. Jewell has selected Kahoot as her tool of choice. She has grouped her students in threes, and their task is to work together to provide evidence to support their responses to questions about mathematical statements that ask them to determine if the statements are always true, sometimes true, or never true. When creating the Kahoot game, Ms. Jewell takes advantage of the option in the game to extend the length of time allowed to answer the questions. This is because she purposefully is planning the task to include time for the three students to come to consensus on their answer and to also record evidence of support and to make their thinking visible. For example, when the first statement appears, "two thirds is two of three pieces," Group A's work might look like this:

Bryan: Yes, two-thirds is two of three pieces.

Roberta: What if one piece is massive, and one piece is small, and one piece is tiny?

Beth Ann: Good point, so we have two examples that show this statement is sometimes true. So quickly, draw a picture that shows our thinking, and I'll select B: Sometimes True on our device.

Let's look at one final classroom before leaving the topic of digital tools to collect student responses.

In Mr. Stephens's classroom, he uses Google Slide Decks to create a gamelike environment to nurture mathematical conversations. To begin, Mr. Stephens first considers how he might move from asking closed questions with one right answer to open questions with answers worth talking about. He found a great resource in Christopher Danielson's inspired website created by Mary Bourassa at http://wodb.ca. Mr. Stephens uses an image from Bourassa's website to stimulate a number talk. The students use the Comments feature within the Google Slide Deck to determine which number doesn't belong and why. Also, students may respond to their peers' comments and challenge their thinking by beginning their comment with, "I disagree and this is why. . . ."

Another important attribute response tools bring to the teaching and learning environment is the opportunity for the teacher to use the students' responses to inform instructional practices. This is truly a transformative moment in teaching and learning! The more efficient the teacher becomes with response tools, recognizing the strengths and weaknesses each tool offers, the more effective the impact will be for the learners. We must make sure that form follows function and that we know the tools thoroughly enough that they then support the richness of open-ended questions.

We are often asked by teachers "*How* do I make learning more relevant and engaging?" and "*How* do I increase student personal response?" Hopefully, this chapter has presented some *how*. But as we close the chapter, we want to present one final thought by Peter Block, author of *The Answer to How Is Yes*.

There is depth in the question "How do I do this?" that is worth exploring. The question is a defense against the action. It is a leap past the question of purpose, past the question of intentions, and past the drama of responsibility.

> The question "How?"—more than any other question—looks for the answer outside of us. It is an indirect expression of our doubts. . . .
>
> —Peter Block (2013, p. 234)

Reflection

Considering the Block quote above, and Hattie effect size findings in Figure 5.16, what summative truth can you write using the phrase *my classroom* or *our school* and any two of the following: *task, question, powerful*? Please write a sentence of truth.

FIGURE 5.16 Two Specific Effect Sizes From the Work of John Hattie

Influence	Effect Size
Teacher: questioning	0.48
Teacher: self-verbalization/self-questioning	0.64

http://resources.corwin.com/powerfultask

CHAPTER 6

Engaged in *What*?

The Power of Cognition

What number would you put in the box to make this a true number sentence?

$$8 + 4 = \square + 5$$

Falkner, Levi, and Carpenter (1999) gave this problem to 30 elementary-grade classes ranging from first grade to sixth. The responses are shown in Figure 6.1.

Understanding equality is essential for students in order to grasp basic arithmetic concepts as well as later on as they begin to develop algebraic reasoning skills. As we consider the response data, it appears "many students have serious misconceptions about the meaning of the equal sign as a relation between two equal quantities. Many seem to interpret the equal sign as a command to carry out a calculation (the answer is . . .)" (Faulkner et al., 1999, pp. 232–326).

And yet, each learner brought an "understanding" to the task. As we analyze how it is possible that the majority of students in each grade cluster chose the incorrect answer of 12, we should first look at the question the learners sees in the task—and has perhaps seen most frequently. As the students read from left to right, they see a very familiar task and answer the question "What does eight plus four equal?" They do not slow down to consider that

FIGURE 6.1 Percentage of Students Who Responded With Each of Four Alternatives

	Response - Percent Responding			
	7	12	17	12 and 17
Grades 1 and 2	5%	58%	13%	8%
Grades 3 and 4	9%	49%	25%	10%
Grades 5 and 6	2%	76%	21%	2%

the real question is "How can we make this equation true?" or "What can we put in the box to make both sides balanced and equal in value?"

$$8 + 4 = \square + 5$$

In terms of engagement, filling in the blank is just a compliant response—most certainly an automatic response by fifth grade—to the placement of numbers and the location of the equals sign and box. The work is neither meaningful nor about students making meaning. That is precisely why the habit of "something plus something equals answer" becomes the student default.

After realizing her fourth-grade students were almost all operating with this misconception, Mrs. Brooks decided to do a little research. She found the writings of John Van De Walle and LouAnn Lovin (2006), who recommend using "balance scale variables" with students so that they might manipulate and literally see and develop the concept of equating two qualities. With this research in mind, Brooks designed a cognitive task for her students using an electronic manipulative from the Illuminations website (https://illumina tions.nctm.org) created and administered by the National Council of Teachers of Mathematics (NCTM). The Pan Balance tool helps students build up to algebraic thinking using shapes of unknown weight. There is a second version of the tool on the website that uses numbers sentences in establishing equality. While that tool more closely resembles the equation students had just encountered, Mrs. Brooks decided to use the representation of the shapes to prevent her students from jumping back down into rote computation. She believed the visual of the shapes would be cognitively more powerful.

Mrs. Brooks explained the activity to her students as follows:

> Today we are going to be using the Pan Balance tool to try to find equivalent sets of shapes by placing shapes on each side of the balance. The pans move according to which side is heavier and which is lighter. When both sides of the pans balance, the equivalent relationship is added to the right-hand table. This is when a prediction can be made as to how much each shape weighs. You will need to capture two screenshots, one showing the pans balanced and one of your Guess Weights screen. Then pull both images into Explain Everything, and explain your thinking as you complete the Guess Weights screen. Write equations to describe what you did.

We would invite you to explore the website to play with your own concepts of equality. The link to the website can be found on the companion website. We think you will find the website both visually and physically interactive, which will enable us to achieve our goal: cognitive interaction and cognitive engagement for our students.

Working in pairs over the next few days, the students recorded all of the equalities they could find and turned them into equations. Mrs. Brooks then used a similar interactive on the NCTM Illusions website to get "back down" in the curriculum to pick up the numerical equalities that had provided the original problem. With their new understanding of the concept of equality, the student were able to do the fill-in the box operations accurately.

> The effective use of manipulatives—both physical and virtual—helps learners make connections between concrete objects and abstract mathematics. In *Visible Learning for Mathematics*, Hattie et al. (2017) describe this as "a surface learning technique with an eye toward deep learning, in that the use of manipulatives bridges students' learning as they move from surface to deep" (p. 126). But the surface-to-deep learning doesn't just magically happen when we put manipulatives in the hands of our students. It is only through thoughtful task design that we are able to bring about and see that the transition from surface to deep has occurred.

The equalities example is a perfect opening to this chapter as we look at two big ideas: cognitive demand and finding balance (pun intended) between the thinking levels as students really learn some content and concepts.

COGNITIVE DEMAND

To be clear, we consider the cognitive demand of a learning task, not the cognitive possibilities. *Demand* refers to the minimum level of cognition required of all learners in the learning moment. It refers to a "floor" rather than the "ceiling." Many students will answer a closed question and open it for more meaningful dialogue and discussion. We are fortunate if we have these students in class, but they bring the engagement and the deeper thinking, rather than the task requiring it.

Let us consider the morning routine in kindergarten as students get settled in. Mr. Rash asks typical questions that only require a Level 1 recall response: "Who brought lunch to school today? Who will be eating the cafeteria food?" The answers from the carpet are quite varied:

"I have a HUGE apple in my lunch bag!" (analysis?)

"Breakfast is the most important meal!" (evaluation?)

"People cook their food, but animals just eat whatever they find wherever they find it." (comparison?)

In every class, somebody always wants to make the learning more engaging and more personal. Sometimes, it's deep thinking, and sometimes it's just that Mr. Rash said the word *cafeteria*.

Now, let us consider balance in learning. As teachers, we want our students to have the ability to work through and across the desired content for full utilization of that content. This would include memorizing facts, names, and vocabulary; as well as making connections between ideas; using information and processes in new, unfamiliar situations; and extending, questioning, and creating beyond the content.

Before we can plan for such a variety of learning tasks, we must have a common language for this work. For decades, schools have struggled to find the right vocabulary to describe, capture, and then plan for different types of learning and thinking. Unfortunately, developing an organizational structure to describe the function of an organ as complex as the human brain is no easy task.

One of the most comprehensive efforts was begun by Benjamin Bloom, Max Englehart, Edward Furst, Walter Hill, and David Krathwohl in 1948. They began by recognizing that the brain operates across three domains: cognitive, affective, and psychomotor. The cognitive domain is concerned with thinking and learning. The affective domain encompasses feelings and relationships, while the psychomotor deals with the brain's control of our physical movements. While a taxonomy (organizational pattern) was developed for the affective domain, it was the taxonomy of educational objectives in the cognitive domain that became the most relevant for educators (Bloom, Krathwohl, & Masia, 1956). The six levels of thinking were defined as (1) Knowledge, (2) Comprehension, (3) Application, (4) Analysis, (5) Synthesis, and (6) Evaluation.

Although Bloom's taxonomy became ubiquitous in undergraduate education coursework, practical application hasn't found its way to most K–12 classrooms. We think part of the reason may be that it wasn't modeled for most preservice teachers. Instead, we memorized the six levels and the concomitant examples and regurgitated them on an assessment (at the knowledge or comprehension level) (Antonetti & Garver, 2015).

The work of Bloom and his colleagues has undergone a number of revisions—each trying to bring additional clarity and application for educators. What we include in the Task Rubric is based upon the revised taxonomy by Anderson, Krathwohl, and Airasian (2001) that rearranges and breaks the taxonomy as (1) Remembering, (2) Understanding, (3) Applying, (4) Analyzing, (5) Evaluating, and (6) Creating.

Anderson et al. further uncovered that each of the six cognitive processes interacts with four different dimensions of knowledge: factual knowledge, conceptual knowledge, procedural knowledge, and metacognitive knowledge. Recognizing these new layers within the taxonomy makes task design even more difficult and complicated for teachers.

When Antonetti and Garver first began their action research on engagement, they quickly realized that ascertaining the level of cognitive engagement of particular students in the middle of a learning task was almost impossible. It certainly cannot be done simply by watching students work; rather, we must talk to them and ask them to explain the task as they experience it. It requires knowing the background knowledge and schema the learner brings into the task, as well as the scholastic opportunities that served to scaffold the task. Accuracy in recording the thinking level is also impacted by the learner's skill in articulating the past, the present, and the future of the learning moment.

While not abandoning the traditional taxonomies, Antonetti and Garver decided to approach the taxonomies from a different angle—that of the learner's current experience with the content. In the current task, does the learner accept meaning from the environment, or does the learner *make* meaning from the environment?

As learners, we merely accept meaning when we take the thought given to us and tacitly agree to make it our own:

- This is a capital letter B and this is the lower case b.
- Living things are classified by the modern system from largest classification to smallest: domain, kingdom, phylum, class, order, family, genus, species.
- The number 2 is greater than the number 1.
- To turn on or wake up your iPhone, hold down the button (shown in the diagram of the start-up guide).
- The largest cities in the United States (as well as the rest of the world) are found on bodies of water.
- The quadratic formula is. . . .
- What an author says explicitly.

To truly *make* the knowledge our own and commit it to memory, we must practice and repeat the accepted meaning.

For example, as learners, we can also make meaning in these ways:

- Put your hand in front of your lips and make a "b" sound and then a "p" sound. Describe what happens with your hand.
- Read the characteristics of the duck-billed platypus. In which class would you place it and why?

- What is a number that is much larger than 127? What is a number that is just a little bit larger than 127? How do you know?

- What happens if you push more than one button at a time?

- Consider the 12 largest cities in the United States. What generalizations can you make about their geographical location?

- Could a quadratic equation have solutions that are exactly 3 apart? What could the equation be?

- What does the author say implicitly?

As teachers and lesson designers, we struggle (and always should) with the best way for students to interact with content: Should they accept meaning or make meaning? Thus, we are always struggling with the efficiency of delivery versus the efficacy of design.

> A reminder: A moment of making meaning should eventually create accepted meaning.

Accepting meaning versus making meaning is—perhaps—a simplistic lens to use, but it works well for teachers and lesson designers to connect engagement and cognition. Let us reconsider the six levels of what is often called the revised Bloom's taxonomy with that lens inserted.

LEARNING THROUGH ACCEPTING MEANING

Remember (Recall)

The learner is presented meaning and accepts it as true. In actuality, "remembering" is the ability to bring information forth as needed.

For example, spelling tests, math facts, elements of the periodic table, and dates in social studies are examples of recall. There is no personal response.

We use the word *recall* in the Task Rubric to capture remembering as well as retrieval. In both cases, there is an already-acceptable bit of knowledge expected by the task. "List the five rights guaranteed by the first amendment to the US Constitution" might be recall of past cognition or the act of retrieval of accepted meaning from a colleague, a parent, a book, or a search engine.

Understand

The learner accepts meaning (or uses a long-accepted meaning) and restates the accepted learning through paraphrasing or providing other examples.

"Give another example of personification." Schema, language, and cultural background become an initial level of Personal Response. In other words, your version of the accepted meaning may be different from that of others in our class because we each lead different lives. Nonetheless, our thinking probably remains very close to the originally accepted thought. "Draw what freedom of speech means to you" is an example of demonstrating understanding.

THINKING AND MAKING MEANING

Apply

The learner uses accepted meaning in a new situation. Personal Response occurs as the learners first make sense of what is new and then consider what to bring forth from the past.

For instance, students have been taught and have practiced how to calculate the area of a rectangle when given the width and height of the rectangle. As students continue to practice calculating area with assorted rectangles, the cognition remains at the understanding level—repeating the procedures while only the measurements (numbers) change. There is not yet a new situation.

As we move into a task of apply, the students are now given the area of a new rectangle as well as the width. They are asked to find the unknown height. To be clear, the making of meaning occurs because they cannot simply repeat the known or accepted procedure. They must make meaning as they decide on how to manipulate the known procedure or how to use other relationships to attack this new problem.

In a traditional approach to building content, *apply* is the "first" level of cognition that brings forth a rigorous task. (More on that in a bit.) To make sure we are truly designing tasks at this level, we can think about our students' current level of understanding and ask ourselves two questions about the task at hand: "What is new?" and "What is you?" In other words, there must be something about the task that is unfamiliar or just outside their known classroom experience, and the task must require each student to make his own meaning in the new situation.

When we ask the question, "Do we have the five rights in our own school," the "new" is thinking about the first amendment from the perspective of the day-to-day operations of a school. This information cannot be "retrieved"—it must be newly formulated.

"Share examples from school life of each of the five rights/freedoms in action (or give examples of how these rights are not protected in school)." Sharing examples from school life is also the "you," as each learner will have different experiences at school upon which to draw. The "new" look at the rights and the personal response of "you" will allow students to see that the rights are not black and white. The question is opened for them to interpret what each right entails and what limits there are to those freedoms in a school setting.

> Ask students: What is "new"? What is "you"?

In our area example above, the student who recognizes that the second type of problem "is just backwards from the ones we've been doing" has just articulated the "new" and proposed her "you" plan of procedural attack.

Analyze

The learner makes meaning by finding patterns, similarities, hypotheses, and truths. We have already discussed (in the section in Chapter 4 on Generating and Testing Hypotheses) that making meaning can happen when learners simply look at something until they discover what is occurring in the content. Our questions of checking for rigorous design flip in order: "What is you?" followed by "What is new?" In this case, "Here's what *I'm* seeing" becomes "Look what I found." This is the essence of Personal Response. In his book *Student Voice* (Quaglia & Corso, 2014), Dr. Russell Quaglia proposes that the desire to make meaning of the world around us is a condition called curiosity. Surely analysis is the beginning of the curiosity.

Unfortunately, the verb *analyze* is used often in task design and results in assignments in which students do not get to make meaning—even if they want to. For example, consider the two tasks in Figure 6.2 as we analyze a William Wordsworth poem.

John often pulls this activity out of his toolkit when he is working with secondary math educators. The minute he mentions analysis of poetry, math teachers groan (the same way English teachers do when they approach a math problem). John usually corners the loudest grumbler and asks, "Why would you not be interested in—or even excited about—analyzing poetry?" The response is typically, "Because I never saw what the teacher saw in the poem."

Before you look at each task with an eye toward its cognitive demand, please answer this question: Which task would you rather complete? Why? How does your expectation of success within each task play into your answer?

If we now look to the cognitive demand, Task #1 demands only a Level 2. If you know that a simile is a comparison of two things using the word *like* or *as,* you can simply circle every *like* and *as* and check to see if it forms a comparison. Likewise, we can find more examples of metaphor and personification. We could find them all! And make 100% on this task! And do it all without Personal Response. And do it without analysis. And without rigor.

Granted, a number of students would take Task #1 to a higher cognitive level. They would gladly connect the figurative language to meaning, tone,

FIGURE 6.2 Analysis of William Wordsworth's "Daffodils"

Daffodils	Task #1:
I wandered lonely as a cloud That floats on high o'er vales and hills, When all at once I saw a crowd, A host, of golden daffodils; Beside the lake, beneath the trees, Fluttering and dancing in the breeze. Continuous as the stars that shine And twinkle on the milky way, They stretched in never-ending line Along the margin of a bay: Ten thousand saw I at a glance, Tossing their heads in sprightly dance. The waves beside them danced; but they Out-did the sparkling waves in glee: A poet could not but be gay, In such a jocund company: I gazed—and gazed—but little thought What wealth the show to me had brought: For oft, when on my couch I lie In vacant or in pensive mood, They flash upon that inward eye Which is the bliss of solitude; And then my heart with pleasure fills, And dances with the daffodils. —William Wordsworth	Analyze the poem for figurative language: Identify the similes, metaphors, and personification by stanza.
	Task #2:
	Analyze the mood of the poem: What emotion does Wordsworth evoke as you read the poem? Be sure to include how he brings forth this mood.

Source: "The Daffodils." Wordsworth, William (1807). Creative Commons License: CC BY-SA 3.0 https://creative commons.org/licenses/by-sa/3.0/deed.it

and mood. They would do this because they are capable, because they are interested, and because they want to increase their Personal Response to the text. As we have said before, we are looking at the cognitive demand of the task, not the voluntary opportunities for thinking.

While the question underlying Task #1 is closed, Task #2 begins with an open question of Personal Response: How does the poem make you feel? In classrooms and workshops, students as young as fifth grade (and math teachers as old as 60) have explained to us how the author's word choice made them feel as shown in the following list:

joy	happiness
introspection	reflection
melancholy	purpose
hope	spirituality

That's eight different personal responses to the poem. Shouldn't that be the reason to read poetry—to connect with the poet on a personal level?

MAKING MEANING ON TOP OF MEANING

The upper two orders of thinking and cognitive demand occur when students use accepted or made meaning to go further in their Personal Response. Students have a tendency to feel more comfort—and will expend more cognitive and constructive energy—in either *evaluating* or *creating*. *Evaluation* continues to be a critical thinking structure based upon the Latin root *crit* (judgment), while *creating* is the creative thinking in a content.

Evaluate

The learner is asked to make meaning and justify claims of comparative or superlative value. By definition, evaluation is deciding that something has more value than something else. "Read these two short stories and write a five-paragraph essay that answers the question 'Which is scarier?' Please note that you may first have to decide what makes a story scary. Use examples from both texts."

When students are operating in the higher level of evaluate, their decision making goes beyond analysis. Typically, however, they must use the truths, patterns, and criteria that were established at the analytical level as they decide what is *-er* or *-est*.

Create

The learner manipulates, combines, or ignores patterns to build a new idea. Personal Response is at its most intense as learners create. Intellectual/Emotional Safety is also incredibly important at this level, as learners will take big risks in their thinking and production. They will actually decide what truths or expectations they will maintain and what

> By definition, there is a bit of rebellion in creating.

they will choose to do in unexpected ways. By definition, there is a bit of rebellion in creating.

Creating starts at analysis—seeing patterns, finding the status quo, and knowing what your audience expects. It then flips as the learner builds the unexpected. Quaglia and Corso (2014) look at the relationship between analyzing and creating through the eyes of a toddler, where analysis is the curiosity to see and make sense of the "why?" "what" and "how?" They then link curiosity to creativity:

> Creativity—the Condition that inspires the ... 3-year-old to mix and match socks or try a tutu for a stylish headdress. Creativity is expressed with the questions "Why not," "What if," and "How else?" (2014, p. 95)

Tasks of cognitive creation involve the student making a new meaning of the learning content. The cognitive demand of *create* does not mean "produce something that demonstrates lower cognition". For example, making a movie about imperialism in a history class does not mean the students were cognitively creating new understanding of the concept of imperialism. It means they put their creative energy into a movie. In some cases, products and presentations are so closely "rubric-ed" that the learners simply follow the production steps or recipe. We will not recognize that as *creating*.

In art class, students are asked to find what makes the work of Van Gogh and Seurat unique, then create a painting that combines the styles of those two artists. The painting itself is not the creative product—the style the student uses represents her act of creation.

In an English class, students are asked to write and perform a poem about teenage life in the 21st century. When it is Tony's time to present, he stands before the class and says "I am a teenager. In two-thousand eighteen." He then sits in a chair for three additional minutes, staring at his phone Nobody was expecting that!

SLIDING ACROSS THE COGNITIVE CONTINUA: A HIERARCHY, NOT A SEQUENCE

Regardless of the researchers or authors, cognitive taxonomies are almost always recognized as hierarchies of thinking. That is, each level builds upon the prior level. Personalized understanding builds upon accepted knowledge; creating happens when the creator decides what to apply, combine, or ignore.

While this certainly makes sense, it becomes problematic. One of the biggest misconceptions we discover when we work with teachers and schools in Task Design is the idea that hierarchy translates into sequence. It is true that each level supports learners and scaffolds activities to bring them to the next level; this does not mean, however, that our lesson sequence must follow the hierarchy. In other words, we can design tasks that skip around in terms of cognitive demand (or slide back and forth across the Task Rubric.)

Let's visit a kindergarten class that is in the middle of a context clues lesson. Mrs. Mullis asks the students to consider a page from Harriet Ziefert's *Hats Off for the Fourth of July,* a text about a patriotic parade (see Figure 6.3).

After reading the first page of text, she stops and tells the children that they are going to use context clues to figure out what the word *twirlers* means. The students in the classroom are well versed in this strategy—they know that analyzing and figuring out is more important to readers than knowing every word, so those students who know what *twirlers* means put their hands on their heads so they won't "take away the thinking from their friends!" Mrs. Mullis reads the first sentence slowly: "The twirlerssssssssss are walking down the street." She asks, "Did you hear that? At the end of twirlerssssssss? Let's read the first two words together. The twirlers. What did we just read at the end of twirlerssssssss?" The students all recognize the -s at the end of the word. "What have we learned about the -s at the end of some words?" Students collectively shout out: "More than one!" (Level 1 accepted recall).

Moving quickly to a Level 3 application, Mrs. Mullis then asks, "So, we know that there is . . .

"MORE THAN ONE!" from the carpet

"Yes, more than one, so (pointing to the unicycle) could this be twirlers?"

FIGURE 6.3 A Page From *Hats Off for the Fourth of July*

NO! from the carpet.

"How do you know?"

Donnie: "There's only one man."

"Could this be twirlers?" (circling the group of three in the background)

YES! from the carpet.

"How do we know?"

Allie: "There's more than one. There's three."

"Great vocabulary work, Allie. Could this be twirlers?" (circling the group of four in red with her finger)

YES! from the carpet

"How do we know?"

Fran: "Because there's more than one. There's four."

"Excellent vocabulary work, Fran. Could this be twirlers?" (pointing to the dog)

NO! from the carpet.

Leah: "There's only one."

"Great, so these (circling the group of three) and these (circling the group of four) could be twirlers. Now let's read a bit more: The twirlers are walking down the street. Partner A, turn and tell you partner who the twirlers are using our context clues. Partner B, tell your partner who are not the twirlers using our context clues."

Our Level 3 application of content clues (and some analysis of the illustrations) gives us a definition of *twirlers*. This will become a Level 1 accepted vocabulary word by the time we finish reading the story, but it moved across the continuum. More important than the vocabulary word, the students used a Generating and Testing Hypotheses approach—using context clues—to make meaning.

As they play with the next vocabulary word—*strut*—they will be unable to completely ascertain the meaning of that word from the text and illustration provided, but they can certainly generate hypotheses!

When we recognize that thinking demand can move across the continuum, we must also recognize that there is a natural progression "backwards" when students get a chance to make meaning. What they discover and then use and practice becomes Level 1 *remember* thinking with time.

The First Amendment lesson sequence presented in Chapter 2 moved across the cognitive hierarchy one level at a time. Since we were building toward the objective of the interaction between the five rights to give us the version of freedom we enjoy in the United States, a sequence that moves upward through the cognitive demand levels made sense as we worked from the acceptance of the amendment to the analysis and evaluation tasks across the rigor divide. The learners accepted meaning and used it to make additional meaning—increasing the Personal Response as we moved into more rigorous tasks. This works well in most content areas.

MATH COGNITION AND THE TASK RUBRIC

If we are not careful, mathematics—and other disciplines and courses that are heavily dependent on procedure and correct answers—may actually train learners to avoid Personal Response or discount their own making of meaning. In the eyes of learners, the more proficient I become at plugging into the correct formula or algorithm, the less likely I am to apply Personal Response and reasoning to my mathematical tasks. (Recall the equality issue from the beginning of this chapter.)

To that end, we found it helpful to use a different taxonomy when considering task design in math classes. We use the task analysis guide developed by NCTM's Margaret Schwan Smith and Mary Kay Stein (1998) (see Figure 6.4). This tool helps teachers inspect and design tasks in four categories of cognitive demand: memorization, procedures without connections, procedures with connections, and doing mathematics.

In 2010, the National Governors' Association and the Council of Chief State School Officers released the final Common Core State Standards in Mathematics and English Language Arts (www.corestandards.org). One of the most exciting components of the math standards was the publication and inclusion of eight Mathematical Practices in each grade level. Mathematical Practice #1 (www.corestandards.org/Math/Practice/MP1/) in each grade states that students will make sense of problems and persevere in solving them.

It is important to note that this mathematical practice has two parts and that the part that comes first—in both the language of the practice and in the actual cognition of problem solving—is making sense. Do we really want students to persevere in a problem if they do not first make sense of the problem? This sounds like a recipe for stress and lifelong math anxiety.

For this reason, we adjust the language of Smith and Stein's fourth domain, "Doing Mathematics Tasks," to "Making Sense." A math task that has a cognitive demand of "making sense" requires complex thinking that is not algorithmic. The underlying question of such a problem is certainly open at multiple entry points.

THE TASK ANALYSIS GUIDE

Lower-Level Demands	Higher-Level Demands
Memorization Tasks	**Procedures with Connections Tasks**
• involve either reproducing previously learned facts, rules, formulas, or definitions OR committing facts, rules, formulas, or definitions to memory.	• focus students' attention on the use of procedures for the purpose of developing deeper levels of understanding of mathematical concepts.
• cannot be solved using procedures because a procedure does not exist or because the time frame in which the task is being completed is too short to use a procedure.	• suggest pathways to follow (explicitly or implicitly) that are broad general procedures that have close connections to underlying conceptual ideas as opposed to narrow algorithms that are opaque with respect to underlying concepts.
• are not ambiguous—such tasks involve exact reproduction of previously seen material and what is to be reproduced is clearly and directly stated.	• usually are represented in multiple ways (e.g., visual diagrams, manipulatives, symbols, problem situations). Making connections among multiple representations helps to develop meaning.
• have no connection to the concepts or meaning that underlie the facts, rules, formulas, or definition being learned or reproduced.	• require some degree of cognitive effort. Although general procedures may be followed, they cannot be followed mindlessly. Students need to engage with the conceptual ideas that underlie the procedures in order to successfully complete the task and develop understanding.
Procedures Without Connections Tasks	**Doing Mathematics Tasks**
• are algorithmic. Use of the procedure is either specifically called for or its use is evident based on prior instruction, experience, or placement of the task.	• require complex and nonalgorithmic thinking (i.e., there is not a predictable, well-rehearsed approach or pathway explicitly suggested by the task, task instructions, or a worked-out example).
• require limited cognitive demand for successful completion. There is little ambiguity about what needs to be done and how to do it.	• require students to explore and understand the nature of mathematical concepts, processes, or relationships.
• have no connection to the concepts or meaning that underlie the procedure being used.	• demand self-monitoring or self-regulation of one's own cognitive processes.
• are focused on producing correct answers rather than developing mathematical understanding.	• require students to access relevant knowledge and experiences and make appropriate use of them in working through the task.
• require no explanations, or require explanations that focus solely on describing the procedure that was used.	• require students to analyze the task and actively examine task constraints that may limit possible solution strategies and solution.
	• require considerable cognitive effort and may involve some level of anxiety for the student due to the unpredictable nature of the solution process required.

OCTM, Professional Development Cadre

Smith & Stein (1998)

Consider the following problem:

Dylan broke open his piggy bank and found a pile of quarters, dimes, and pennies. He had a total of 52 coins. He used all of his coins to buy a book for $5.98. As he was stacking up his coins to pay the clerk, he realized two of the stacks had the same number of coins, while the third stack had twice as many coins. How many quarters, dimes, and pennies did Dylan have?

Since we have not done so for awhile, we invite you to begin to make sense of this problem in the space provided below. You may choose to complete the problem, or you may give up before getting to a solution. Either way, make some sense.

Because there is no one expected entry into this problem, students will bring their personal response as they determine the best way to get started. (Most students will only see one way—their way—into the problem.)

Mari honed in on the "twice as many" in the third stack and drew the picture in Figure 6.5:

FIGURE 6.5 Mari's Approach

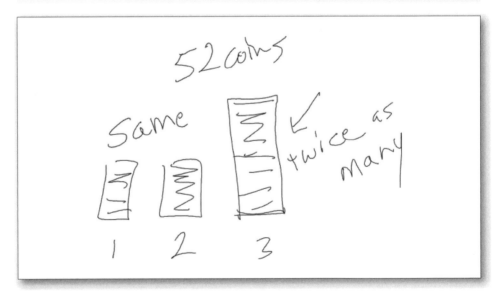

FIGURE 6.6 Derrick's Approach

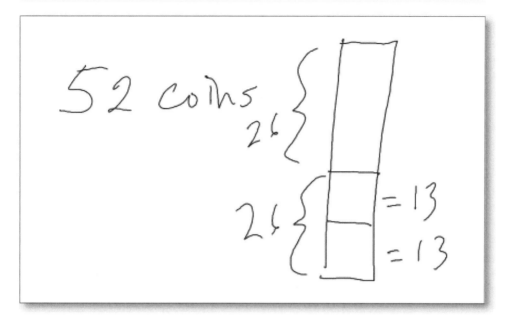

Derrick began to think about all of the coins together (Figure 6.6).

Samantha divided 5.98 by 52 coins and found the "average coin" was 11.5 cents. She then reasoned that most of the coins were quarters (Figure 6.7). Since half of 52 is 26, she tried 27 quarters and then got stuck.

FIGURE 6.7 Samantha's Approach

$$5.98 \div 52 = 11.5¢ \leftarrow \text{more}$$
$$27 \times .25 = 6.75?$$

Leona divided 52 by 4 and got 13. She found the value of 13 quarters and then 26 quarters. She then added 13 dimes to the 13 quarters. This is where she was when we walked away from her desk (Figure 6.8).

FIGURE 6.8 Leona's Approach

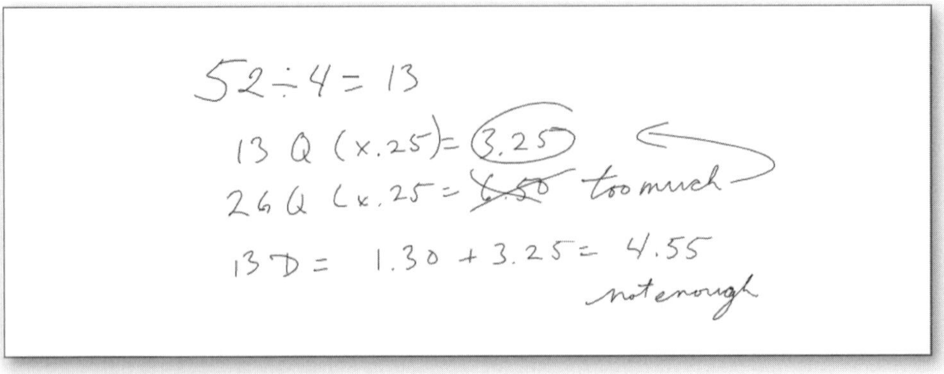

$$52 \div 4 = 13$$

13 Q (x.25) = ⟨3.25⟩ ←

26 Q (x.25 = 6.50 *too much*

13 D = 1.30 + 3.25 = 4.55

not enough

The task design demands that each student *make sense* at a Level 4. As some of the students develop their attack, they certainly may apply procedures that are familiar and may actually fall back to *procedures with connections*. But the entry into the task is still a Level 4, since there is no expected algorithmic way to solve this problem—unless the teacher models a similar problem first. If that were the case and the adult taught the steps of solving this scenario, the cognitive demand would be reduced to a Level 2.

And now we are back full circle to why mathematics should probably not work "up" from Level 1 to Level 2 to Level 3. Such an approach kills cognition at a Level 4.

As much as we value Smith and Stein's task analysis guide—and Bloom's taxonomy, for that matter—we must add an important caveat or caution. The first is about implementation. As teachers ourselves, we have found that we sometimes design tasks of higher cognitive demand only to "overteach" them, removing the rigor during implementation. Another version of this rigor reversal occurs as students begin to struggle and we ask guiding questions of our students: "Would it be helpful if you first determine how many coins are in each of the stacks?" (In other words, "Could you please use the strategy that I would use if I were making sense?")

For this reason, we must witness students as they are involved in the task so we can check for possible "rigor slippage." Analysis of student work—or of lesson plans—is never as accurate as actually watching learners engage in (or compliantly work through) a task.

An Additional Continuum of Cognition

We include in the Task Rubric a continuum based upon the work of James Webb and his Depth of Knowledge framework (Webb, Alt, Ely, Cormier, & Vesperman, 2005). The top band of the rubric (Figure 6.9), showing the cognitive demand of the task, reflects their work. This framework was designed primarily for aligning testing with standards and not for planning instruction. It is more about the cognitive opportunities a task might allow. It is typically considered a "ceiling" expectation when students are asked to perform a task that measures learning, rather than to meet a demand during learning. We do not believe it lines up as neatly as depicted within the rubric, but it does share some interesting parallels with Bloom's taxonomy and with Smith and Stein's task analysis guide. We present it in the rubric simply as another powerful consideration in analyzing student work and in planning cognition during learning moments or assessment of learning.

FIGURE 6.9 Powerful Task Rubric—Top Band Showing Cognitive Demand

	Power Component	1	2	3	4
Cognitive Demand	Bloom – Revised Taxonomy *Examples*	Recall Name the steps	Understand Follow the steps	Apply/Analyze Infer with text support	Evaluate/Create Argue, defend, or justify
	Antonetti/Garver/Stice – Meaning	Repeat accepted meaning	Restate or reproduce accepted meaning	Making meaning: Find patterns Find use for patterns	Compare patterns Add/combine/ ignore patterns
	Webb – DOK (Assessment)	Recall	Skill/Concept	Strategic thinking	Extended thinking
	Stein/Smith – Mathematics	Memorization	Procedures without connections	Procedures with connections	Making sense

ENCODING AND MEMORY

As a summary thought, we reference a statement by Jan de Fockert,

> When presented at encoding, motivation can affect memory (de Fockert, Rees, Frith, & Lavie, 2004, p. 758).

Rather than simply accept that meaning, we wish to move through a Level 2 cognitive task and restate it with Personal Response:

> When students are interested in the content or the process during moments of making sense, memory increases.

And now our own thought (Level 3 cognition, Generating a Hypothesis, *explaining or defending our idea*):

> The earlier in the lesson sequence we can have students working across the rigor divide, the better the cognitive retention.

And finally, to turn this idea into a bumper sticker:

> Get 'em across the divide as fast as possible. Better yet, trust the learners and start there.

REFLECTION

In what ways does the information about student cognition validate what you believe and practice in your classroom?

What in this chapter is a new consideration or challenges your beliefs and/or classroom practice?

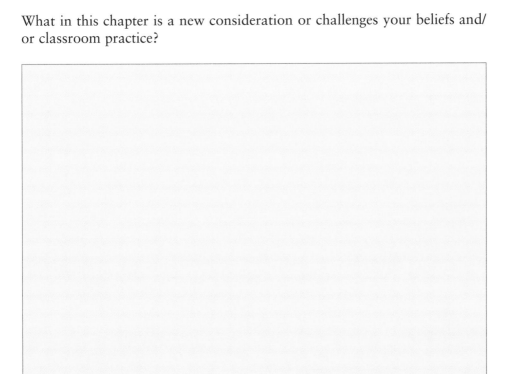

CLOSURE

To wrap up this chapter, we encourage you to scan the QR code to the companion website to access Video 6.1, a video created by a seventh-grade middle school student named Charlie. In the video he explains how he was able to lower the heartbeat of his Doberman, Rosie, and stop her from wolfing down her food by petting and talking to her.

While we advocate using the Powerful Task Rubric to analyze the task *design* and the requisite learning, in this case, we do not actually know the expectations of the learning task. Please use the evidence provided in the video to analyze *Charlie's* learning as revealed through the Powerful Task Rubric. Think about the science and the thinking separate from the quality of the presentation. Perhaps we should consider the learning task and the production task as two separate pieces.

http://resources.corwin.com/powerfultask

CHAPTER 7

Power Up

Using the Diagnostic Instrument to Analyze Learning

If we want to change our practice, we have to practice the change.

If you are reading this book, we can assume that you are interested in increasing learner engagement, shoring up student thinking, and improving student achievement. But before we start revising our lesson plans and redesigning our tasks, we have to make sure the tasks should be reworked. A task of practicing verb conjugations is a necessary task in a world language class. It will not, in and of itself, build a fluent bilingual adult, but without conjugation practice, the adult will not be proficient in that language. We say this and mean it: Not all tasks should be powered up—some learning remains only at the accepted and practiced levels.

If the task and the concomitant learning do merit a redesign, we must decide what in the lesson design needs to be reworked. If we are being asked to make our instruction more engaging, we must first decide what part of the standard or outcome elicits engagement. If we are adding more rigor to our tasks, we must make sure that we power up the right part of the standard and use the appropriate continuum from the Task Rubric to leverage that power. Our goal is not to simply make the task longer or harder.

A couple of years ago, we had the opportunity to work with Matt, a high school principal who chose to move to an elementary school so that he could learn more about the K–12 continuum while working on his superintendent's certificate. Matt shared that the district had asked him to work on rigor in the new elementary school. In one of our training sessions with primary grades, Matt shared his struggle: "I'm not sure how we make everything more rigorous. For example, how do you make things like tracing letters and cutting on the line more rigorous?"

John could not resist the chance to have just a quick moment of fun. "To make cutting more rigorous, you hold the paper and walk backwards while

> Sometimes we need to let things be what they already are.

the children follow you and try to cut on the dotted line." In all seriousness, Matt was voicing a struggle that we all must face—what is worth making rigorous?

Most of our work in schools starts with a school's stated desire to increase student engagement in classrooms. While this is certainly an admirable—and desirable—goal, we must be careful. We often remind teachers that curriculum trumps instruction. Or to say it another way, curriculum matters more to achievement than instruction—it dictates the cognitive demand of the learning tasks and often provides the "why" for the learner. If a school has not done the alignment work between standards, curriculum, and assessment, we can spend significant time and energy on better instruction but end up with a school filled with engaged learners, making meaning of the "wrong stuff" while high-stakes test scores begin to slip.

THE DIAGNOSTIC INSTRUMENT TO ANALYZE LEARNING

To avoid spending energy and money in professional development that will not move the learners, we must be diligent and thoughtful in determining the focus of our adult learning and continuous improvement cycles. In 2006, Antonetti and Garver developed an analytical tool to help schools develop meaningful staff development plans—and avoid just jumping onto the next PD bandwagon. The tool is known as the DIAL, the Diagnostic Instrument to Analyze Learning. The DIAL allows us to use assessment data to determine the focus of the professional growth for a grade level, a PLC, a school building, or even an entire district.

A special note: If you are a statistician by trade or passion, please be warned that while we are about to present a highly practical tool based upon solid research, it may cause some trepidation for readers who prefer numbers and data to people.

PREMISES AND RESEARCH BEHIND THE DIAL

> Premise #1 The bell curve does exist in reality.

It has, in the past 20 years, become taboo to speak of the bell curve (Figure 7.1) in education. That is as it should be as we maintain high expectations for all learners and deliver competency-based instruction. However, outside of school—in any random group of 100 people—interests, experience, and motivation place us in different positions on the achievement continuum. For example, John is an avid gardener and his yard has been awarded national display garden status for the American Hemerocallis Society (day-lilies). We could say that John is in the top 10% of gardeners. Terri is an Apple Distinguished Educator and Google Certified Teacher. We could say that Terri is in the top 10% of ed tech practitioners. And yet, we both continue to learn and seek out expertise in our areas of interest.

On the other end of the achievement spectra, John is in the bottom 10% of golfers and Terri is in the bottom 10% of seamstresses. Whether suggesting strength or weakness, our current placement on the bell curve is NOT our destiny. Indeed, thinking that it might represent our future is the hidden danger of spending too much time considering—or giving credence to—the bell curve as a model in learning situations. Given time and appropriate learning tasks, Terri could become a skilled seamstress and John could become highly adept with a 9 iron.

FIGURE 7.1 The Bell Curve

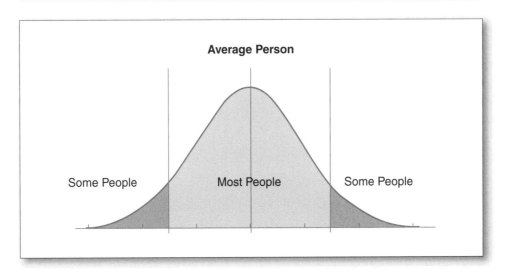

Let us now extend the bell curve premise to this (perhaps offensive) hypothetical teaching scenario: John presents a one-hour lecture about daylily hybridizing techniques to a captured (but polite) audience of 100 people. For the participants, there are no embedded tasks during the presentation—they only listen. At the end of the seminar, each participant takes a 10-question, multiple-choice assessment of the learning. It's not hard to imagine that the results would fall into a "normal curve" picture of achievement. A few highly motivated or highly interested listeners might get all 10 questions correct—scoring 100%. The bored or disinterested might only get one question correct, but the majority of our listeners would fall somewhere in the middle, and we can probably expect a mean score of 50%.

For those of you who have jumped ahead in your thinking about this scenario, yes, we could certainly shift the achievement on the daylily test if the teaching included more than lecture—or if there were actual, visible student learning tasks during the hour. We'll come back to this in a bit. For right now, please just accept how our achievement data fits the normal curve.

Premise #2 Curriculum trumps instruction.

In his seminal work on curriculum and assessment, Dr. Fenwick English (1999) discovered some interesting mathematical patterns in achievement data. One of the most impactful ideas is the ability to quickly see the big picture in our data and to determine whether our weaknesses are curricular or instructional in nature. Knowing this can help us avoid falling victim to initiative overload or jumping into the next training that may or may not impact achievement.

When we have access to criterion-referenced data, we can plot that data onto a bell curve that is rotated onto a vertical axis, with the four quartiles representing the percentage correct or points "earned" by a group of students. According to English, the lower the scores drop below the 50% correct or earned level, the more likely the issues are curricular in nature. English proposed that the achievement drop was the result of students not having access to the intended curriculum—perhaps it was not taught or the teachers assumed the learner already had sufficient baseline knowledge or experience. Another issue that causes the bell curve to slip below the 50% level is that the content "taught" was not aligned to the manner in which it was assessed.

As a caution, this premise only holds true when we plot hard numerical data—as in the percentage of students correctly answering a question, or total points earned out of points possible. Achievement data that represents "contrived" categories—such as percentage proficient—uses arbitrary cut-offs and is not *as* mathematically reliable for use in this tool.

To illustrate the English premise, the graph on the left in Figure 7.2 shows the "expected" normal curve on an assessment. If our actual data included a mean score of 29% on a particular standard, objective, or outcome, we can hypothesize that we have a curriculum or alignment issue rather than an instructional issue. The curve on the right of the figure shows how this lack of access to the intended curriculum pulls the achievement curve down.

If we consider Dr. English's premise in our working example, we might be cautioned to consider the content of the daylily lecture and its relation to the

FIGURE 7.2 Expected Normal Curve of Scores on an Assessment

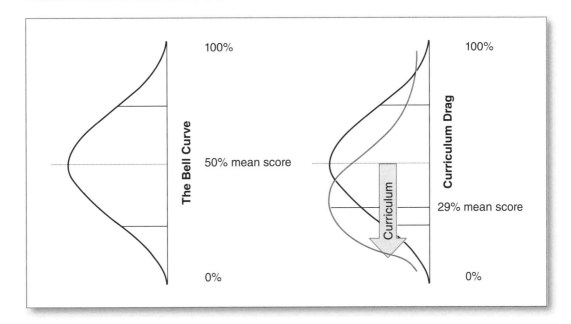

assessment items, before we make changes to instructional delivery or task design. In other words, if we have not sufficiently done our curriculum work, changing how we teach or how learners experience the content may not result in better achievement. Do we know that the daylily presentation even addressed the items tested on the exit? What if the lecture was on the history of daylily hybrids, but the test asked the listeners to classify types of daylilies?

Most of us did not enter the education profession to work on curriculum. When young children "play" school, you rarely hear a child say, "Hey come on over to my house. We'll get together a PLC and dig deep in the verbs of our curriculum documents to determine the assessment targets. It will be so fun!" And yet, without the foundational curriculum work, we may simply spin our instructional wheels.

Premise #3 We must guarantee curriculum and access for all.

Larry Lezotte, the founder of the consulting organization Effective Schools, summarizes the work he and his colleagues have done in a profound statement: "One of the best kept secrets in education is that students do tend to learn what it is they are taught in school" (1992, p. 35).

If we add this idea to the bell curve and the work of Fenwick English, we can then hypothesize that if we truly taught the content that was to be tested, we should not see the mean on an evaluation slip below the 50% mark. Another issue uncovered in Effective Schools research is that kids who come from affluent homes actually inflate achievement because of experiences outside of school.

To isolate the impact of the school on curriculum and instruction data, we do not plot the scores of the entire student population on the DIAL. We only plot the aggregate scores of students of poverty. This minimizes or nullifies the impact that experiences brought from home might have in covering up or masking the true picture of our school's impact on learning. We might have a mean daylily score of 50% that is actually inflated because just over half of our participants have taken field trips to the botanical gardens, have access to the community greenhouse, or are themselves botanists; while the other half of the participants live in concrete tenement apartments and have no prior knowledge of lilies.

> **Premise #4 Task predicts performance.**

As Antonetti and Garver conducted their research in 17,000 classrooms, they were able to capture and identify trends regarding learning tasks. These Look 2 Learning visits provided the leading indicators of achievement—what students were doing in the learning moments. After the fact, Antonetti and Garver were able to compare and correlate their data to the exit data from state assessments, college placement exams, and end-of course tests. They found that each of their "look-fors," or problems of practice, could predict a drop in test scores in the specific quartiles or bands of achievement.

To illustrate this correlation, let's revisit the poetry class example from Chapter 1 in which students identified figurative language in a poem rather than analyzing the conveyed meaning and tone. When students took the district assessment, they earned only 29% of the total points on figurative language. If we place this data point on the DIAL (Figure 7.3) and compare it to the words on the left side of the DIAL, we see that a score of 29% falls near the "objective" component from the L2L protocol. This suggests that the learning tasks did not give students access to the actual standard, intended objective, nor the required cognitive demand (Bloom). It might also speak to text that was above the current reading level (On Level). In other words, we have a curriculum issue rather than an instructional issue: the *what* in the learning task was off, rather than the *how* of the learning task.

USING THE DIAL

Working our way up from the bottom of the form, we begin with **Standard**. This is just what it appears to be—does the task match the standard (or scaffold to the standard)? It is important to be especially mindful that trend data may illuminate that we spend significant time on tasks that are scaffolding toward or are subskills of a standard, but very little time with students actually performing the standard.

Next is **On Level**. This is alignment to the vertical scope and sequence of the standard.

Objective refers to students' ability to explain what they are asked to do, what they are learning by doing said task, and why or how they will use what they are learning in the future.

The fourth look-for is **Bloom** and refers to the alignment between the expected cognition (from the standard) and the cognition of the task at hand.

These first four components are all a part of *curriculum*. Typically, they are already delineated by the state, province, school district, or other governing body.

In the middle of the DIAL, we place the **TASK**. The task is the first part of the instructional side of the teaching-learning cycle. We place it at the 50% mark, as this is the transition from guaranteed curriculum to viable curriculum. It moves the curriculum to the learner and is the first place where a teacher's design and professional choices should come into play. As English discovered the relationship between a drop below 50% and a failure to teach the required curriculum, we have discovered that as scores move closer to 50% and continue higher, the next levels of learner growth will come from redesigning tasks for increased **Engagement** and student-controlled **Strategies**.

The final component level is **Personalized Learning**. When our students of poverty are approaching 75% of the points possible, we should allow them to take control of their learning. Technology plays an even more important role in this arena.

On the left hand side of the DIAL are corresponding questions we must ask about our practice based upon the location of the data points.

We are now ready to use the DIAL.

THREE DIAL IMPLEMENTATIONS

Figure 7.3 shows a DIAL data page that includes assessments of six different concepts/standards at three different schools.

At Westside Intermediate School, where we regularly visited math classrooms throughout the second semester, we saw students working on fractions in fifth-grade math classes using the curriculum materials purchased by

FIGURE 7.3 DIAL Form With Three Examples

Data Analysis

Look 2 Learning

Diagnostic Instrument to Analyze Learning

Percent of Students Mastering Standard/Item
Percent Correct on Criterion Referenced Assessment

Questions to Consider								
	100	100	100	100	100	100		
Are we fostering independence?	95	95	95	95	95	95		
	90	90	90	90	90	90		
Can learners take control?	85	85	85	85	85	85	Personalized Learning
	80	80	80	80	80	80	
	75	75	75	75	75	75	
Are high yield strategies visible?	70	70	70	70	70	70	Strategies
	65	65	65	65	65	65	
Is work authentic and engaging?	60	60	60	60	60	60	Engagement
	55	55	55	55	55	55	
	50	50	50	50	50	50	TASK
Is the cognition matched?	45	45	45	45	45	45	
	40	40	40	40	40	40	Bloom
Is it accessible to students?	35	35	35	35	35	35	
	30	30	30	30	30	30	Objective
	25	25	25	25	25	25	
Is it aligned to standards?	20	20	20	20	20	20	On Level
	15	15	15	15	15	15	
Is this in our curriculum?	10	10	10	10	10	10	Standard
	5	5	5	5	5	5	
	Westside Grade 5 Fractions	Eastside Writing "Claim"	Eastside Writing "Evidence"	Eastside Writing "Organization"	Eastside Writing "Conventions"	Northside phase changes	L2L

Standard or Concept Assessed

the school site council. What we noticed during our visits was that the tasks seemed to be the same tasks from fourth grade. The students were successful practicing the skills, but there was an alignment issue. When the scores came back from the state, the data showed that the students (of poverty) had an average percentage correct fraction score at 28% (rounded up to 30%). If we look at the placement of that score in the numerical grid, we see that it lines up just above the On Level impact component. The DIAL is telling us that our issue is curricular. Before we work to make the task more rigorous or more engaging, we should first dig into the standards and make sure our students are actually learning and practicing the fifth-grade version of fractions. We should ask ourselves, "Is our work aligned to the fifth-grade standards?"

At Eastside Elementary School, second-grade teacher Paulette Feraldi received the scores for her students' on-demand district writing prompt. The writing task required students to make a claim about a character in the short passage they had just read. As soon as she received the scores, she converted the class averages to percentages to place on the DIAL. These are shown in Figure 7.4.

When she placed the four scores on the DIAL, what first jumped out to her was that "using evidence to support claim" was falling into a curricular consideration (43% rounded up to 45%). The second thing she noticed was the correlation to Bloom's taxonomy. Mrs. Feraldi hypothesized that per-haps her students were not thinking at the appropriate cognitive level in this part of the work. As she reread the papers, it became clear that students were simply copying parts of the text or retelling the story rather than finding the "best" evidence to support their claim.

And here is where the DIAL and the Powerful Task Rubric come together. The DIAL suggested to Mrs. Feraldi that she should somehow power up the task of finding evidence in the text. She recognized in the Task Rubric that

FIGURE 7.4 DIAL Scores for Mrs. Feraldi's Classroom

School: EES	Grade: 2	Teacher: Feraldi
Scoring Domain		
Making a claim		3.1 78%
Using evidence to support claim		1.7 43%
Organization		2.6 65%
Conventions		2.5 63%
Weighted Writing Score Average		2.5

her students were simply accepting thoughts the author presented instead of using the author's words to explain and support their own ideas. She decided to push her task cognition to a Level 4 Evaluate.

For the next few weeks, students in Mrs. Feraldi's class were given a claim about a character in a book they had read previously during the year, and the students worked in groups to find and quote at least three pieces of evidence that supported the claim. The children then worked in groups to rank the evidence quotes from weakest to best.

Mrs. Feraldi chose to work on this cognitive part of the reading-thinking-writing task rather than have her students write entire papers. Two weeks later, she gave the students a parallel writing cold prompt. Her student "evidence" scores rose to an average of 2.9 (73%).

At North High School, students in Mr. Wen's chemistry class have been reviewing states of matter and phase changes—content that they also learned in eighth-grade science. When he gives his first test, the students do poorly on the short answer required by Question #11, in which they must explain how pressure on and temperature of molecules impacts state and phase changes. Only half of the students provide the correct short answer. As he places the score of 50% (the class earned 50% of the total points possible for this item) on the DIAL form, Mr. Wen is reassured that the taught curriculum is solidly aligned with the assessment item. He also recognizes that a reteach must involve powering up the learning task. The DIAL further suggests that the powering up should incorporate engagement and strategies. (If we consider the Look 2 Learning components on the DIAL as rungs of a ladder, powering up the instructional task means to reach above the current zone of achievement.)

Mr. Wen remembers a website he saw in a science meeting that he thinks will provide the tasks he needs. He puts his students into pairs and has them download a phase change simulator from the PhET Interactive Simulations project at the University of Colorado Boulder (link found on the companion website).

The directions to the students are simply,

> You have 15 minutes to play with this simulator. You must answer in writing the question, "How do applied pressure and temperature impact state changes?" We will ask for volunteers to share their answers and you will use the simulator to test the truth of their findings.

When this task is analyzed on the Task Rubric, it is evident Mr. Wen pushed the students into rigor by powering up the technology to take control and manipulate the simulator. At the same time, he has the students Generate/Test Hypotheses by identifying and articulating patterns and relationships through their analysis of the visual. Finally, as the first volunteers share their findings, there is Learning With Others, as the other teams will have to recreate and prove—or revise—the shared findings.

A week later, Mr. Wen interrupted the new unit of study with a pop quiz asking the same Question #11 from 10 days prior. On that day, 92% of the students were able to successfully articulate the relationships among pressure, temperature, and phase changes.

TIPS FOR THE TOOL

In designing a tool, form must follow function. The Diagnostic Instrument to Analyze Learning is about reflection, conversation, and finding direction. It can validate our work and suggest our next steps for continuous improvement. It can make our lives easier and make our teaching more effective.

At the hardware store, even the simplest power tools have warning labels literally glued to the side of their packaging. Here is our warning label: This tool is not to be used to cause emotional harm, to injure or scare teachers. With that in mind, here are some final utilization reminders:

1. *Plot data that will give the most insight into the task and curriculum.*

Plotting and analyzing vocabulary questions 14, 15, and 16 is more helpful than looking at the "vocabulary acquisition through context clues." We can use the information we get from the DIAL to decide if we truly taught context clues or if the issue was we did not do it at the right level of text complexity. In mathematics, we will get more accuracy in identifying our next steps in the classroom if we plot "variable and expressions" rather than "algebraic computation."

2. *Plot any data that is a numerical percentage.*

An individual teacher might plot the percentage of students who got each particular question right on the end-of-unit exam. (Forty-two percent of students correctly answered question #14, identifying the type of conflict in the literary passage.) Again, drilling down to this level will provide the most accurate picture of reteaching needs. A high school science department might choose to plot the percentage of points earned by the total student population on a particular topic on the common assessment. For example, if the test had four questions on modeling cellular growth, and all eleven class sections took the assessment, we might plot that the student body earned 67% of the possible points from the aggregate. This is broader view of our current practice and is not the same thing as the average achievement percentage, but it still may provide the department with some important information as we prioritize reteaching or revising our instructional tasks. We must keep in mind, however, that as we move further away from specific questions, we may inadvertently cover up some issues that would be visible if we could drill down to each test item. Moving even further away from specificity and accuracy, we must be careful if we are tempted to plot data regarding proficiency levels. These levels are typically artificial "bands" or reporting categories of achievement rather than accurate mathematical statements of learning. A statement that 71% of our students are proficient in number sense does not mean that 71% of our students got every number sense question right. The label of *proficient* might only require a student to correctly answer 10 out of 15 questions. That said, if all you have available is state assessment data regarding proficiency levels, the DIAL can still provide the right conversation starters for the PLC and can lead the teaching team into plausible next courses of action.

3. *Plot data that represents your low socioeconomic students.*

These are the students who are dependent on us for curriculum and instruction. Do not plot special education or English language newcomers. Remember we are looking for foundational next steps. We must consider differentiation after we find our primary achievement issues.

4. *When planning focus areas for development and staff work, reach "up the ladder" of the current achievement level for growth, but make sure that those indicators below the current level of achievement are solid.*

Our final chapter in this book presents 27 tasks for your consideration. These tasks represent a wide range of grades and disciplines. They come from schools across the country. We do not consider them examples or exemplars. They are solid tasks designed by consummate professionals. We do not judge them, but we learn from them.

We can learn how technology engages learners. We can find tasks that are high in cognitive demand, yet, we may still need to power up the learning task by leveraging an additional continuum from the Task Rubric to pull our students over the rigor divide.

So, let's go. Go, go Power Rangers.

http://resources.corwin.com/powerfultask

CHAPTER 8

Putting It All Together

In *Leaders of Their Own Learning* (2014), Ron Berger, Leah Rugen, and Libby Woodfin write about "building a mindset of continuous improvement." When we first began working together, we made it a priority to always seek descriptive feedback from colleagues as well as our learners. We know a mindset of continuous improvement is critical to our work. Today, we continue to revise our work—sometimes making significant changes, sometimes only minor tweaks, but always with improvement in mind.

Without reservation, our favorite part of the work we do is when we get to be in classrooms with teachers and students. This chapter is about what happens there, the tasks teachers design, and the students who are doing the work.

Neither of us came up through a system that taught us to design rigorous tasks. Perhaps, like the most fortunate of teachers, we stumbled into some great tasks with our students. If we reflected on why these tasks were powerful, we began to realize what made them powerful and used that in our next task design. It is also likely that we sometimes fell woefully short in meeting the potential of our learners or in challenging them to work at the next level.

With this in mind, we recognize that we teachers are a hard-working lot. We master new bits and pieces of pedagogy, technique, and style and continue to build our toolkits by learning from each other. In that spirit of collaboration, all of the teachers represented in this chapter have given us—authors and readers—permission to use and to critique the tasks represented in this chapter. We would encourage you to use their tasks as a starting point for conversations about rigor, engagement, thinking, and strategy. And if at all possible, look at these with a critical friend. Agree with our commentary or disagree. Accept what we think or—better yet—make meaning from the work of 27 colleagues.

Here's how we will present the tasks for your consideration:

> **The Task:** The tasks include samples from multiple grade levels. These are not complete lessons from beginning to end; rather, they capture the smaller learning moments of a task. A high-quality task can always be tweaked and made better.

Student Work: Most tasks include examples of student work, presented here or housed in our companion website. If student work is available, it would be malpractice for us to analyze a task without the student "present," even if we are looking at artifacts and not live learning.

From the Powerful Task Rubric: Here is our commentary. It is neither complete nor the only way to look at the task. It is, instead, what grabbed our attention.

Power Up: Occasionally, we offer our suggestions to power up the task. These suggestions are by no means the only ways that the task could be pushed across (or further across) the rigor divide. Typically we think about adding one Power Component at a time. Sometimes the tweak involves technology, and sometimes the power is without a power cord.

Before you jump into this work, we thank you for reading this book and we are honored that you join us in continuing to learn from colleagues and from the learners in our care.

Prekindergarten students learn to make an argument and back it up with evidence.

After listening to a read-aloud of *Hey, Little Ant* (via YouTube), the students reviewed the pictures in the book, analyzing which pictures supported stepping on the ant and which supported not stepping on the ant. Then each student made a claim: Yes he should step on the ant, or No he should not step on the ant. Using an iPad and the Explain Everything app, the students captured three pictures to support their claims and recorded their explanation of their ideas.

Student Work Samples on the Companion Website

From The Powerful Task Rubric

The technology allows kids to "think bigger than they are able to write." The product is evidence of Level 3 cognition (*apply/analyze with text support*), Level 3 strategy (*make unique decisions about content*), and Level 3 Personal Response (*explain and support my ideas*). Rigor at age 4!

During library time for kindergarten, first-grade, and second-grade students, we began with a read-aloud of a book. Then students broke out into centers where they had a different task to complete at each center. Students rotated through the centers.

Reading and Understanding Center: Working in small groups, students completed a graphic organizer about the story. Students analyzed how a character develops and changes throughout the story.

Retelling Center: Working in small groups, students reenacted the story using puppets. Students had a copy of the book with them at the puppet theater so that they could go to the text and look for the action in the story. Students improvised and made up alternate endings.

Research Center: Working in pairs, students researched using an online database, PebbleGo, and explored a topic of their choice.

Words Center: Working in pairs, students used the Osmo Words game on an iPad Mini to guess and complete vocabulary words from the story.

From the Powerful Task Rubric

The most cognitive task of the center rotations is the one students complete at the Reading and Understanding Center. The students are not simply retelling the plot but determining how the character changes over time, connecting character traits, motivations, and feelings, as well as plot points (cognitive demand Level 3). In the Retelling Center, the students are working at a lower cognitive level as they retell plot points and the story event; however, when they improvise and come up with an alternative ending, this can push the cognition across the divide—especially if they logically connect the new ending to the plot or character development presented in the story. If, however, the new ending is completely disconnected from the story (Red Riding Hood calls Batman to fight the wolf) we might need to examine the Personal Response to determine if it is simply a product of David's love of superheroes or a true understanding of the story . The Research Center provides a space for students to take *control* of their own learning, and their interests will power their learning (technology Level 3). The Words Center is a gaming approach to spelling vocabulary words. The cognitive demand is low, but the Novelty and Variety make the task fun. An important point to note is that sometimes students are working alone in the centers, sometimes in pairs, and sometimes in groups.

Power Up

Technology can power up the Reading and Understanding Center, if we allow students to take pictures of the character before the change, during the change, and after the change. Then they can bring the pictures into the Explain Everything app and describe the change as well as the most important event(s) that cause(s) the change.

Students developed their own math problems for their parents to solve.

Students created a Chatterpix video to deliver their math problems to their parents. As the teacher shared the videos with each student's parents, she asked the parents to provide a wrong answer or solve the problem incorrectly, so that students could "correct" their parents. The students then analyzed their parents' strategies for solving the problem and provided feedback to them via Explain Everything.

Student Work Samples on the Companion Website

From the Powerful Task Rubric

Technology allows the Novelty and Variety and Sense of Audience within this task to shine. The Personal Response in building the problem is at a Level 2: *fill in the blank with my answer*. Listen to students' feedback to parents to determine whether the cognition is a Level 2 *procedures without connections* or a Level 3 *procedures with connections*.

The students individually worked on a math problem, choosing the strategy that made the most sense to them.

Later in the week, they used an online video creation tool (www.animoto.com) to make a video (*products*) to show their work. The videos were posted on our class website.

Student Work Samples on the Companion Website

From the Powerful Task Rubric

In Chapter 3 we discussed how this task has many engaging qualities—some that cross over the rigor divide and some that stop short. Since this is the first time the students encounter a problem of repeated addition or grouping, the cognition is at a Level 4 *making sense.* There are multiple entry points in attacking this problem.

Power Up

While the cognition starts at a Level 4, the production of a video overshadows the mathematical thinking, as making the video is more fun. To make sure the video incorporates the thinking, students could upload a picture of the strategy they used to solve the problem and explain their thinking in a voice-over. This addition to the task would allow the students to share their mathematical thinking with the world (technology Level 3). Personal Response now crosses the rigor divide when students explain their ideas (Level 3).

After reading two versions of The Three Little Pigs—*The Three Little Pigs* and then *The True Story of the Three Little Pigs*—students formed an opinion as to which story they believed to be true. They explained why they believed it to be the true version using details found in the book.

Then students used Chatterpix to capture a picture of the cover of the book they believed to be true and recorded 30-second explanations defending their answers.

Student Work Samples on the Companion Website

Powerful Task Rubric

With the use of technology, six-year-olds in the first month of school are able to have a Personal Response at a Level 4 as they explain and justify their ideas. The Novelty and Variety is also at a Level 4, which is evident as we listen to their *perspective.* The technology is at a Level 3, which puts the learners in *control, sharing* the their thinking with others. The cognitive demand of this task is at a Level 4 as students decide which text better supports the truth. The students are *personalizing and making unique decisions* about the content (Level 3-4 Summarizing). It is interesting to note the students sticking to their opinion rather than retelling the whole story.

Power Up

As the students progress to articulating and supporting their opinions in writing, we can expect that the physical act of writing may diminish their Personal Response. Letting students record their thoughts as they did, and then using that as a dictation exercise, might give us better writing.

Students planned a field trip for three second-grade homeroom classes to travel to and from Mammoth Cave National Park, located in Mammoth Cave, Kentucky.

Students were provided the following information: number of students in each class, the name of the tour they would be taking at Mammoth Cave, and the date and times of the event.

From the Powerful Task Rubric

The power of this task is the authenticity and relevance of planning a field trip. The cognition begins at a Level 4 as the students determine what information they need (how many seats on the bus, how many miles of travel, etc.) and the best way to find it.

The students solved the following problem using any strategy they were familiar with and wanted to use.

Problem:

You have $10 to spend on chocolate, but the store only has Hershey bars ($2 each) and Tootsie Rolls ($1 each). How many ways can you spend *all* your money without getting any change back?

After the students found a way to solve the problem on paper, they used Explain Everything to make their thinking visible to all stakeholders.

Student Work Samples on the Companion Website

From the Powerful Task Rubric

While there are six combinations of candy that will result in all of the money being spent, this question only has one right answer—six ways in all. It is an open question in terms of how students enter the problem and identify all of the possible combinations. There are multiple ways to enter the problem and multiple ways to represent all of the ways to spend the money—some children draw pictures, some make a table, and some use tally marks. The openness of the question provides a cognitive demand of Level 4 (*making sense*), as students explain and support their ideas at a Level 3 of engagement. The technology is at a Level 2, as all of thinking has already occurred and the learner is just using it to record. However, it is valuable to both the learner and the teacher as we hear and see each student's approach to solving the problem.

The students work in groups to complete the slope intercept form, following these directions:

Use the "Explore" tool within Google Docs to determine exactly what the term *slope intercept form* means and to establish the formula that represents it.

Next visit www.desmos.com/calculator and type the formula for slope intercept into a new Desmos activity. Use the slides to investigate what the variables do. Insert Screenshots into the table cells, and explain what you discover.

From the Powerful Task Rubric

This task is predicated upon making connections with and between procedures on the slope intercept form (Level 3 cognition). The technology allows students to see how manipulating the equation (Level 3 technology, *taking control*) impacts the graph. The students Generate and Test a Hypothesis based upon their manipulation of the form.

The students were assigned to groups of three or four and given a specific, compound figure to work with.

The group drew the compound figure and showed how they broke the figure into simple shapes, found the area of each simple shape, and found the area of the compound figure.

Next each group was assigned a new compound figure that another group had already worked on. The second task was more challenging because the group had to break the figure apart in a different way than the group before them and repeat the steps from the first round.

Student Work Samples on the Companion Website

From the Powerful Task Rubric

As Mrs. DeJarnette explains in her reflection video, the Learning With Others was a powerful component in the task design. This is not captured in the artifacts of the student work. The student work shows evidence of procedural proficiency with area of rectangle and area of a triangle, but without hearing the students articulate their thinking, we are unable to place the task on the rubric for cognitive demand.

Power Up

By capturing the student talk—using only the technology tool all middle schoolers have in their pocket, we would be able to determine if the cognitive demand of this task crossed the rigor divide. The student talk would also help us determine the impact of Novelty and Variety as well as Learning With Others this task offers. Another possible way to power up is to focus more on the *compare and contrast* of the shape deconstructions and why they both result in the same number for area of the compound figure.

For five minutes of class, students "analyzed" the Rita Dove poem "Testimonial" by marking it in any way they chose to. (There was much uncertainty and looking at neighbor's papers for ideas or affirmation. I loved this part!) Without guidance, the students noticed the structure, speaker, tone/mood, figurative language, literary devices, and meaning.

Now familiar with Dove's style, the students read another of her poems, "American Smooth." The students struggled to make sense of the poet's word choice and imagery.

Then the students were provided with the first two paragraphs of an article that appeared in the *New York Times,* "American Smooth: Dance Fever." These paragraphs provide additional biographical information about poet Rita Dove. The article made the students curious about the American Smooth dance style.

I pulled up a video of a ballroom dance competition featuring the American Smooth style of dance. We discussed what we saw in the video. The students then reread the poem and made connections between the dance style and the author's life. This allowed the students to literally see a poem in a new way.

From the Powerful Task Rubric

The self-described "uncertainty" demonstrates that the literary analysis is truly analysis (cognitive Level 3). Students looked at the text until they decided what they saw. They were not told what to find. The analysis of the second poem was influenced by the biographical information provided by the article. The synthesis of the three sources allowed the students to create a new understanding of the poem (cognitive Level 4). The power of the technology in this task is that it provided an immediate opportunity for students to see what they asked to see (technology Level 3, *interests power learning*).

After reading *Serafina and the Black Cloak* as a novel study, students found evidence throughout the book that helped them to classify *Serafina and the Black Cloak* into multiple genres. The students used Google Draw to create a web; then they identified evidence that justified their inclusion of the novel in each of the genres at a specific location in the web.

From the Powerful Task Rubric

The analysis of the text for evidence of genre is at a cognitive Level 3.

Power Up

If, after completing the analysis, we ask students to choose the genre that "best" captures the text, the cognition moves to a Level 4 *evaluate*. As they *explain their reasoning and summarize their support* from the text, students push the Personal Response and Summarizing across the divide.

After reviewing their own assessment results on the MAP (*Measures of Academic Progress*), students found three academic vocabulary words that caused them to struggle on the test. They added those words to the Master Vocabulary Google Sheet (shared with the entire class).

The students used Google's search engine to find definitions for each of the three words they selected, and then they copied and pasted the definitions into the spreadsheet. Next, students rewrote the definitions in their own words and used each word in a sentence.

Student Work Samples on the Companion Website

From the Powerful Task Rubric

While the cognition is at best a Level 2, this task is built upon Intellectual/Emotional Safety as students articulate their own struggles and then take ownership of what they don't know. The collaborative nature of the Google Sheet allows students to see other students with similar vocabulary gaps. They can *compare* their definitions and sentences with those of their classmates to better clarify the meaning of vocabulary words.

I was planning our literature circle for our upcoming novel study and I asked, Is there anyway I can take our traditional literature circle and make it better with ed tech? The answer was YES! By putting all of the tasks of a traditional lit circle into a SHARED digital slideshow in Google Classroom, I gave my students an opportunity to communicate and collaborate simultaneously.

The key to this assignment is making sure you give students editing access when you upload the assignment to Google Classroom. Having the lit circle in a digital platform gave my students access to supports such as speech-to-text and spell check. The level of creativity was heightened because students had access to digital design tools in the slideshow.

From the Powerful Task Rubric

While traditional lit circles provide great opportunities for students to interact with their peers, teachers are often unable to manage full participation of each member within each group. Adding technology to the traditional lit circle provides visible evidence of students' thinking, both within their assigned roles and as they work with other learners (*interdependence in roles or mini tasks,* Level 3). The students are providing feedback in written form (*interdependence of ideas,* Level 4). At the same time the efficiency of the tool provides the teacher "proximity" to all of her learners, and she can provide feedback as they need it.

The original lesson may be found here: http://teachingkidsnews.com/2012/06/19/4-surprise-thatsjustin-bieber-busking-at-theavon-theatre/.

Students were shown a picture of Justin Bieber with no name attached to it. Then the students individually wrote down everything they knew about the person in the picture. They shared and compared their thoughts with their elbow partners. If students learned anything new, they added it to their lists.

The students were then given the title of an article about the individual in the picture, "Surprise! That's Justin Bieber Busking At The Avon Theatre." Students answered the following question: "Based on what you know about Justin Bieber, what do you infer that he has been caught doing?" And based on what evidence?

Next, students read the first two paragraphs of the article on the website Teaching Kids News (www.teaachingkidsnews.com) and determined if their inference turned out to be true.

Then they wrote an answer to this question: "Whenever Justin Bieber performs, he sings to thousands of adoring fans. So why do you think he decided to busk to a small group of people passing by?"

From the Powerful Task Rubric

This is a reading activity of Generating and Testing Hypotheses. The first time students are asked to infer, it is without text support, and they are provided very little information. If they do not know the meaning of *busking,* they jump to a conclusion about its meaning based on their background knowledge or opinions about Justin Bieber (*restate or reproduce accepted meaning,* Level 2). The second time students are asked to infer, they all have a guaranteed base knowledge provided by the article (*apply/analyze,* Level 3, *infer with text support*).

2-5-8 Choice Menu

Directions: Choose two activities from the menu below. The activities must total
10 points. Place a checkmark next to each box you choose to show which activities you will complete. Have fun!

2 POINTS – Knowledge & Comprehension

❑ Summarize what you learned about Immigrants by creating a cartoon.

❑ Locate a map relating to American Immigration during the late 1800s and early 1900s. Explain how natural resources, available jobs, and climate might have contributed to locations in which immigrants chose to settle.

❑ Identify the five most important artifacts you discovered during our primary source Detective Station by disguising them in a hidden picture scene.

5 POINTS – Application & Analysis

❑ Apply what you've learned about Immigration to create an informational brochure that persuades future immigrants where to settle. Make sure to highlight the most attractive features and aspects of your area to attract new citizens!

❑ Create a Venn diagram analyzing the similarities and difference between why immigrants came to America in the late 1800s and early 1900s and reasons individuals wish to immigrate to America today.

❑ Prioritize the top four important reasons immigrants come to America. Create a commercial using these reasons to persuade individuals to move to your area!

8 POINTS – Synthesis & Evaluation

❑ Produce a flipbook from the perspective of an Immigrant. The pages should focus on the same categories from our Clue Graphics Organizer.

❑ Evaluate the perspective of immigrants coming to America in the late 1800s as well as the perspective of America citizens using the primary sources located in our Google Classroom and the Detective Station. Choose one perspective to defend and design a digital mini-lesson to teach your peers about this perspective.

❑ Make a digital comic strip that evaluates and includes the perspective of both an Immigrant coming to America and an American citizen.

Student Work Samples on the Companion Website

From The Powerful Task Rubric

While the Powerful Task Rubric only identifies seven engaging qualities, the original Engagement Cube featured an additional quality—*choice*. Choice of task is not included in the Powerful Task Rubric since the tool is about analyzing or planning a single task. Mrs. Wilder offers her students a menu of nine tasks in this lesson entry and allows her students to decide which tasks they will complete. Giving students a choice *among* tasks provides the student with a sense of ownership and *control* of their learning. Choice does not, however, automatically influence the other elements in the rubric. We would encourage our readers to analyze each of the tasks on the Task Rubric for it's specific power. Mrs. Wilder offers her students a number of choices to demonstrate their *analysis* of the primary sources.

The students created a concept map that included all critical vocabulary terms as well as representative pictures of the terms that demonstrated their understanding of how changes to physical and biological components of an ecosystem affect populations.

One of the biggest issues with this task was that some of my students were unfamiliar with concept mapping format. They just wanted to write down words, draw a picture around said words, and then connect the words with lines. So, I had to back up and model what a concept map is supposed to show. I used a simple topic of sports, and together we built a concept map. Once the students were clear on the expectations, they seemed to understand the premise of the assignment.

I felt that this activity was a little more engaging than a straightforward study guide for a summative test. The students enjoyed trying to come up with pictures for the ecology terms and sharing their maps with each other.

Student Work Samples on the Companion Website

From the Powerful Task Rubric

The standout quality in this task is its visual nature. As we consider the Nonlinguistic Representation strategy, we can see that students place terms into a pictorial form. More important than the images they choose to draw is their placement of the images and their demonstration of relationships among those images. With only the student work as evidence, we can guarantee the strategy is at a Level 2 (*place into other forms*), but without the kids explaining their maps, we may not know if they *created new representations* of concepts and relationships. In other words, we cannot ascertain whether they mapped accepted content relationships or conceptualized relationships within the content.

Power Up

Once again, if we used a technology tool all middle schoolers have in their pocket to capture the student talk while sharing, we would be able to determine if the cognitive demand of this task crossed the rigor divide. If the students are able to explain and support their ideas of placement and direction of arrows, we would be able to determine if the cognitive demand crossed to *pattern finding* (Level 3) or remained at *restate* (Level 2).

To start a unit on food preservatives and genetically modified organisms, Ms. Sheffield went down to the local butcher and purchased a pound of fresh ground beef, from which she made hamburger patties. She also purchased a hamburger from a well-known fast food restaurant. After cooking one of the fresh patties, she presented the two hamburgers to the class. The students had to individually write predictions about what would happen to the burgers if they were left out in the classroom for a week, and why they thought their predictions would come true.

When the students arrived in class the next day, they were greeted with the foulest of odors. What could it be? The students revisited their original predictions and revised them if they felt that was necessary. They then hypothesized about the odor.

- Student #1 hypothesized the salt in a fast food burger kept it from rotting.
- Student #2 proposed there were chemicals in the fast food burger.
- Student #3 thought the thickness of the burger made a difference.

When one volunteer came forward to investigate, he discovered the smell was coming from the cooked hamburger made from freshly ground beef. The fast food burger seemed to be just as it had been the day before. How could this be?

From the Powerful Task Rubric

This is an example of Generating and Testing Hypotheses (Level 3). In writing, students are *explaining and supporting their ideas,* revising or validating them as new information is discovered. Students asked the teacher when the fast food burger would rot. The students convinced her to leave it out for the next couple of days. She agreed as long as they would make another prediction as to when they thought it would rot.

Do your ears hang low?

Students looked at several pictures of animals, including fennec foxes, elephants, jackrabbits, dogs, and horses. For each animal, they described its ears.

Then they answered the questions, How do the animals' ears differ from each other? and Which animal do you think has the best hearing ability?

Each student then chose an animal she thought could hear the best and provided a hypothesis for why this animal had the best hearing. The students found other students who had chosen the same animal, and together they prepared an argument using what they knew about the animal to explain why their animal had the best hearing.

Students rolled paper into an inner ear cone after the teacher demonstrated how. They placed an electronic PASCO sound sensor at the narrow end of the cone to measure the sound levels received inside the cone. With an audio recording of human voices playing across the room, the students measured the decibel range of sounds within the cone.

To test their original hypotheses, students cut paper to form the pinnae (outer ear) shapes and features of their chosen animal, and taped this to their inner ear cone. Again, they placed the sound sensor at the point of the cone and recorded the decibel range for the same audio.

The class recorded the sound levels for each of the animals under consideration in a class document. Students were then asked to revisit their original hypotheses and answer the following questions:

Which animal did you choose at the beginning of this exercise to have the best hearing? Do you still think your hypothesis is true? Why or why not? The students were required to use the evidence gathered from their experiment to make their argument.

Finally, the class was presented with an image of a slit-nosed bat and asked to use what they had learned to predict how that mammal's hearing would compare to the hearing of the other animals investigated in the task, and why it would be better or worse.

From the Powerful Task Rubric

This task is a perfect example of Generating and Testing Hypotheses. It is a solid Level 3 in thinking (*analysis*), strategy (*identifying and extending patterns*), and Personal Response (*explaining and supporting my ideas*). Pay particular attention to the questions at the end of the task. "Do you still think your hypothesis is true?" is a question that builds Intellectual/Emotional Safety for science students, in contrast to the question, "Was your hypothesis right?" The technology component in this task is at a Level 4, *experiment,* providing practice in collecting accurate data and the authenticity of a real science experiment.

Students completed this trigonometry activity in pairs. One student used a Google Cardboard viewer to view screens on the Cardboard website, while the other student read directions. Then they switched roles.

Directions were as follows:

Open Cardboard; follow the directions on screen, and then click on "Urban Hike."

1. Read to your partner: "You should be looking at the Eiffel Tower. Located in Paris, France, it is one of the most well-known structures in the world. The Eiffel Tower is made from iron and weighs around 10,000 tons. From where you are standing, look at the very top while I measure the angle of your chin elevation with a protractor."

   a. You need to measure the angle using the protractor.

   b. Angle measurement: _____

If the Eiffel Tower is 984 feet tall, how far are you from the base?

Have your partner look straight down and click the button to move to Tokyo.

2. Read to your partner. "You are now in Tokyo, Japan. Around 35 million people live in Tokyo; there are so many people most apartments are only 170 square feet. Look at the top of the building that has five different stories. From where you are standing, look at the very top while I measure the angle of your chin elevation with a protractor."

   a. You need to measure the angle using the protractor.

   b. Angle measurement: _____

If you are standing 250 feet from the building, how tall is the building?

The first person is done looking through Cardboard, switch so the second person has a chance.

From the Powerful Task Rubric

The power of this task is in the engagement. Instead of practicing trig calculations with paper and pencil, the students visually travel across the globe (Authenticity) and physically become the measurement components (Novelty and Variety). The cognition remains at Level 2, but now the students are able to see the content in a real-world context.

Power Up

There are two possibilities to power up the cognition.

1. We could ask the learners to make connections between the two procedures within the task, since the problems use different trig calculations. Students could then be asked if it is possible to design a Google Cardboard problem that uses a third trig calculation.

2. We could introduce the trig functions using this activity and allow students to make sense at a Level 4, but it is such a reach for most students that we might want to leave it where it is—an engaging moment of procedural practice.

Students wrote a four-sentence story that marked a historic milestone in their lives. This was followed by a brief discussion, both in small groups and as a whole class, about the event they chose, why it was memorable/worthy of writing about, and why they chose to include the information that they had chosen for their four sentences.

After completing this writing and discussion, students completed the following tasks:

- Students were given a copy of Lincoln's Gettysburg Address via Google Classroom. The document contained the text of Gettysburg Address and was also embedded with a link to an audio version of the speech, so that it could be heard.

- Students were also given an organizer via Google Classroom (a free learning management system) that asked them to chunk the speech based on how it was organized (listing paragraphs or sections). Then they were to determine what the most important information was from each chunk; and finally, they were to reflect on, respond to, or question the information that they had identified as most important in each chunk. This task was completed with partners.

- Once they completed the above task, the partners shared their work with another pair to form a group of four. The students compared responses and then worked collaboratively, as a whole group, to analyze their differences and develop a final copy of the organizer that reflected their new thinking.

- Students then added a "why" column to the organizer in which they reflected on why Lincoln may have chosen to emphasize the things he did and present them in the style he did.

After analyzing this text structure, students used the structure to create their own "addresses" to memorialize the milestones they had written about in their own lives.

Student Work Samples on the Companion Website

Powerful Task Rubric

This is a Level 3 application task in which students *analyze* the structure of the Gettysburg Address and then use what they learned about style and structure as a frame for their own commemorative address. The Novelty and Variety of placing their own story into the structure and style of the Gettysburg Address brought about a *product with concepts* (style, structure, and voice). The use of Google Classroom allowed for Learning With Others and *sharing and providing feedback*.

The students followed contemporary issues and the various ways these issues are portrayed in the media (*The Atlantic, New York Times* Room for Debate, Student News Daily, Newseum, BBC News, PBS News Hour Extra, etc.)

After exploring issues, students created a blog on one issue of their choice, and added articles, videos, and photos to it.

Student Work Samples on the Companion Website

From The Powerful Task Rubric

When students create their own blogs, *interests power learning*. The questions, sharing, and contributions become "breadcrumbs" of their journey to learn the content (technology Level 3). The blog automatically brings Sense of Audience—perhaps to a Level 3 (*an audience I want to appreciate me or my ideas*) or a Level 4 (*an audience I want to influence*). The purpose of blogging is to *explain and support ideas* or *defend and justify ideas* (Personal Response Level 3 or 4).

Students read excerpts from young adult historical fiction novels that were based in the time period they were studying. While reading, students looked at historical themes and details from the excerpts that connected or illuminated the social studies content they were studying. The excerpts were two to four chapters long, and the entire activity took about a 90-minute block, but it gave students a deeper understanding of the historical details.

The students drew pictures to capture what happened in each chapter and wrote a summary sentence.

Working in pairs, the students made connections between the literary works and the history they were studying by identifying the cultural, historical, and political influences on the characters.

From the Powerful Task Rubric

The Novelty and Variety of discovering patterns in literature and connecting them to history results in students seeing the content through a human *perspective* (Level 4 engagement).

Students worked in groups of five with one Chromebook per group. They were asked to list three assumptions about Africa and the basis for those assumptions. Then students read an online article to check their assumptions for accuracy.

From The Powerful Task Rubric

This is the beginning of Generating and Testing a Hypothesis in a human geography class. The task is designed so that students will own their thoughts, including misconceptions about Africa. It is a Personal Response Level 2. From the original Engagement Cube, we could also consider this task an advance question, cue, or organizer that will lead the students into the human and physical geography they are about to encounter. The engaging quality of Intellectual/Emotional Safety is present, since there is no expectation of accuracy, only a collection of assumptions that may or may not hold to be true.

Power Up

To move the Personal Response across the divide we add a Learning With Others component:

Each member of the group grabs three Post-it notes. On each of their three notes, students write one assumption they have about the continent of Africa. Next, members of the group present their assumptions to the others and place their sticky notes in view. After everyone has presented, the group works together to look for patterns/similarities among their assumptions, sort the notes into categories, and label the groupings. For example, a category might be "climate," and an assumption might be "miserably hot." Using the collective knowledge of their group, they eliminate any notes they now realize are not true. Then they write three assumptions they believe to be true.

In a world history class (covering 1400 CE to the modern day), we often do not have time to teach as much contemporary history as we would like. This project is designed to efficiently give students an awareness of more recent events around the world.

Students chose a country through a Google Form utilizing the choice eliminator feature. (Once a student chooses a country, it is removed from the list.)

Students searched the Internet for one "real news" topic for each year between 1990 and 2017. "Real news" was defined as something that happened in their chosen country that made international news.

Students wrote an abstract about each of the events and cited their sources.

Using the information gathered, students then created a timeline of their 27 events (from the 27 years covered).

Using sticky notes, four students recreated and posted their timelines—one on each wall in the classroom. The remaining students then carouseled around the room making connections to their country's events. They added their sticky notes with an explanation of how the events connected.

From the Powerful Task Rubric

The most powerful moment in this task is the carousel activity and the analysis that follows. When students are able to discover and articulate *patterns* (cause and effect, impact, correlation) represented by the sticky notes, they truly see the interconnectedness of our modern world (cognitive demand Level 3). The nonlinguistic nature of the task creates a new representation of interdependence between nations that students rarely see (Level 3). While the technology is at a Level 1, retrieving information with the efficient use of a search engine allowed students to reach the powerful learning moment. Would this task have been possible without the use of technology?

Power Up

With devices in the hands of learners during the research phase of this task, students get into groups of four and explore their countries one year at a time, sharing connections as they go. This would allow students to have the pattern finding along the way as opposed to at the end of the task.

http://resources.corwin.com/powerfultask

Final Thoughts

The journey of our work together has never been about technology first, but only about how technology might improve a well-designed lesson. Our Alaskan teacher contributor, Rylee Ownbey (who authored the literature circle lesson in Chapter 8) said it best in one of her blog posts, "I plan my lessons with standards and students' needs first, and then ask myself: Can I make this lesson better with ed tech?" Sometimes the best use of technology might be something as subtle as the use of a backchannel tool to make the students' thinking visible to all learners, which in return powers up the classroom discussion.

> Master teachers have high skill and high will. They don't just know their craft; they also have the drive and determination to be the best at it.
>
> —Robyn R. Jackson
> *Never Underestimate Your Teachers* (2013), p. 12

Other times, with a single click, the unfathomable happens and connects your work to other like-minded individuals around the globe. It is through powerful task design our students will thrive in a connected learning environment.

In her book *Never Underestimate Your Teachers*, Robyn Jackson writes, "All teaching is a combination of skill and will" (2013, p. 12). She goes on to define *skill* as the science of teaching, stating that "it involves a teacher's pedagogical and content knowledge" (p. 12). Teachers must have both content knowledge and pedagogical knowledge, meaning they must know their content, and they must know the best strategies to help the students learn the content. As important as having the skill is having the will. For it is within the will that the passion for the work of teachers lies, and as a result, they will do whatever it takes to make students successful. We believe if teachers who read *Powerful Task Design* have the will, their skills will improve by making just one change to power up the tasks they design for the learners in their classroom.

When we put devices in the hands of our students, we must do so embracing a hands- and minds-on approach. Technology in the hands of students without a clear purpose is a distraction for all stakeholders in the school community.

It is imperative we approach devices in the hands of students with the mindset that when students' hands and eyes are physically engaged, their minds will be working overtime wondering, questioning, and discovering patterns that lead to predictions and more! As powerful task designers, we can design for these moments, and when the tasks are executed, the minds-on piece will feel like a natural reaction for the learner. We have personally experienced this phenomenon while collaboratively planning tasks for use in workshops and trainings. On multiple occasions, Terri has suggested "John, let's use the See-Think-Wonder routine at the start of the day to get our audience cognitively engaged." We'd find a topic, begin searching, and before we knew it, 45 minutes had passed. In each case, we learned far more than we thought we wanted or needed to know. A few of the questions we asked with see-think-wonder are listed below (just in case you also want to get lost in some fast research):

- Why are axolotls the perfect pet for neuroscientists?
- What fairy tale is most frequently found in cultures and countries around the world?
- Why is the common basilisk lizard know as the Jesus Christ Lizard?
- How do the demographics in our home state compare to past, present, or future trends across the United States?

Because we enjoy getting lost in our curiosity and making meaning, these are the same kind of moments we want to create for our students, tasks that make them want to take control of their own learning, dig deeper, and let their interests power their learning.

A number of years ago, Mr. Lewis Carter, superintendent of Monroe County Schools (Kentucky), invited Terri to speak to the administrators in his school district. Near the end of the meeting, one of the elementary school principals, Mr. Tommy Gearlds, asked her one of the most profound questions she had heard in her 24 years in K–12 education. He first explained, "Terri, I have purchased interactive boards, clicker systems, document cameras, and every other tool I think might help my teachers deliver instruction in the most productive way. Now, here comes the question I need an answer to: "What is it I am supposed to see when I walk into teachers' classrooms that would confirm the money we have spent is worth the investment?" Our pursuit to answer Mr. Gerald's question is what brings us to our current work as described in this book. It is not the physical or social interactions with the technology that we should look for during classroom observations—these are simply classroom behaviors. Rather, we should look for (and celebrate) the cognitively engaging learning experiences of making meaning that students will be excited to tell us about as a result of #PowerfulTaskDesign.

References

Anderson, L. W., Krathwohl, D. R., & Airasian, P. W. (2001). *A taxonomy for learning, teaching, and assessing: A revision of Bloom's taxonomy of educational objectives.* New York: Longman.

Antonetti, J. V. (2008). *Writing as a measure and model of thinking: A mira process.* Phoenix, AZ: Flying Monkeys Press.

Antonetti, J. V., & Garver, J. R. (2015). *17,000 classroom visits can't be wrong: Strategies that engage students, promote active learning, and boost achievement.* Alexandria, VA: ASCD.

Asch, S. E. (1951). Effects of group pressure on the modification and distortion of judgments. In H. Guetzkow (Ed.), *Groups, leadership and men* (pp. 177–190). Pittsburgh, PA: Carnegie Press.

Berger, R., Rugen, L., & Woodfin, L. (2014). Leaders of their own learning: Transforming schools through student-engaged assessment. San Francisco, CA: Jossey-Bass.

Block, P. (2013). *Stewardship: Choosing service over self-interest.* San Francisco: Berrett-Koehler.

Bloom, B. S., Krathwohl, D. R., & Masia, B. B. (1956). *Taxonomy of educational objectives: The classification of educational goals.* New York: D. McKay.

Bruner, J. S., Goodnow, J. J., & Austin, G. A. (2009). *A study of thinking.* New Brunswick, NJ: Transaction Books.

Chouinard, M. M. (2007). Children's questions: A mechanism for cognitive development. *Monographs of the Society for Research in Child Development, 72*(1), vi–ix.

City, E. A., Elmore, R. F., Fiarman, S. E., & Teitel, L. (2009). The instructional core. In *Instructional rounds in education: A network approach to improving teaching and learning* (p. 23). Cambridge, MA: Harvard Education Press.

Danielson, C. (2007). *Enhancing professional practice: A framework for framing. (2nd ed.).* Alexandra, VA: ASCD.

De Fockert, J., Rees, G., Frith, C., & Lavie, N. (2004) Neural correlates of attentional capture in visual search. *Journal of Cognitive Neuroscience, 16,* 751–759.

English, F. W. (1999). *Curriculum alignment.* Thousand Oaks, CA: Corwin.

Falkner, K., Levi, L., & Carpenter, T. (1999). Children's understanding of equality: A foundation for algebra. *Teaching Children Mathematics, 6,* 232–236.

Grossman, L. (2015, July 6). The old answer to humanity's newest problem: Data. *Time, 186*(1), 41–43.

Hattie, J. (2012). *Visible learning for teachers: Maximizing impact on learning.* London: Routledge.

Hattie, J., Fisher, D., Frey, N., Gojak, L. M., Moore, S. D., & Mellman, W. (2017). *Visible learning for mathematics: What works best to optimize student learning, grades K–12.* Thousand Oaks, CA: Corwin.

Jackson, R. R. (2013). *Never underestimate your teachers: Instructional leadership for excellence in every classroom.* Alexandria, VA: ASCD.

Lezotte, L. W. (1992). *Creating the total quality effective school.* Springfield, VA: ERIC Document Reproduction Service.

Marzano, R. J., Pickering, D. J., & Pollock, J. E. (2008). *Classroom instruction that works: Research-based strategies for increasing student achievement.* Alexandria, VA: ASCD.

Medina, J. B. (2014). *Brain rules: 12 principles for surviving and thriving at work, home and school* (3rd ed.). Seattle, WA: Pear Press.

Quaglia, R. J., & Corso, M. J. (2014). *Student voice: The instrument of change.* Thousand Oaks, CA: Corwin.

Small, M. (2017). *Good questions: Great ways to differentiate mathematics instruction in the standards-based classroom* (2nd ed.). New York: Teachers College Press.

Smith, D. J., & Armstrong, S. (2014). *If the world were a village: A book about the world's people.* Toronto, ON: Kids Can Press.

Smith, M. S., & Stein, M. K. (1998). Selecting and creating mathematical tasks: From research to practice. *Mathematics in the Middle School, 3*(5), 344–350.

Van de Walle, J. A., & Lovin, L. H. (2006). *Teaching student-centered mathematics: Grades K–3.* Boston: Pearson Education.

Walsh, J. A., & Sattes, B. D. (2005). *Quality questioning: Research-based practice to engage every learner.* Thousand Oaks, CA: Corwin.

Webb, N. L., Alt, M., Ely, R., Cormier, M., & Vesperman, B. (2005, December). The web alignment tool: Development, refinement, and dissemination. In Council of Chief State School Officers (Ed.), *Aligning assessment to guide the learning of all students: Six reports* (pp. 1–30). Washington, DC: Author.

York-Barr, J. (2001). *Reflective practice to improve schools: An action guide for leaders.* Thousand Oaks, CA: Corwin.

Index

Academic strategies
  engagement qualities and, 63 (figure)
  First Amendment Rights (freedoms) task
    1, 28–30
  First Amendment Rights (freedoms) task
    2, 30–38
  First Amendment Rights (freedoms) task
    3, 38–44
  First Amendment Rights (freedoms) task
    4, 44–45, 46–49 (figure)
  First Amendment Rights (freedoms) task
    5, 50–53
  generating and testing hypotheses, 95–106,
    98 (figure), 101–102 (figure),
    104–106 (figure)
  identifying similarities and differences,
    78–79
  nonlinguistic representations, 91–95,
    93–95 (figure)
  note-taking becoming note-making,
    83–89, 84 (figure), 86–89 (figure)
  Powerful Task Rubric and, 76, 77 (figure)
  reflection and closure on, 107
  reflection in note-making, 90, 91 (figure)
  reflection on tasks, 53–56
  starting on the playground, 75–76
  summarizing and note-taking, 79–83,
    80 (figure), 82 (figure)
Access for all, 161–162
Achievement
  bell curve and, 158–160, 159 (figure)
  curriculum trumping instruction in,
    160–161, 161 (figure)
  guaranteed curriculum and access for all
    and, 161–162
Activity
  listening/watching, 11–12
  as not always a task, 10
  relationship between task and, 11–12
Airasian, P. W., 138–139
Alexander, Mary Beth, 125, 180
Amazon.com, 58

American Revolution, the, 78–79
Analysis and meaning, 142–144
Anderson, L. W., 138–139
Answer to How Is Yes, The, 132–133
Antonetti, John, 11, 13–15, 139, 157–158,
  162, 196
  comparison of similarities, 65 (figure)
  gardening award, 159
Apple iPad, 67
Asch, Solomon, 130
Asking for a sentence of truth
  questions, 126
Authenticity, 62

Bell curve, 158–160, 159 (figure), 161
Berger, Ron, 169
Berry, Amy, 182
Bieber, Justin, 184
Block, Peter, 132–133
Bloom, Benjamin, 138
Bloom's taxonomy, 88, 138
Bourassa, Mary, 132
Braman, Megan, 186
Brooks, Rebecca, 181

Calhoun, Kim, 193
Carpenter, T., 135
Carter, Lewis, 196
Cassidy, Erica, 190
Changing the question, 127
Chouinard, Michelle Marie, 110–111
Classroom Instruction That Works, 78, 85
Closed versus open questions, 124–130
Cognition, 135–137
  closure on, 155
  Depth of Knowledge framework,
    152–153
  encoding and memory in, 153–154
  and learning through accepting meaning,
    140–141
  making meaning on top of meaning and,
    144–145

math, 148–152
reflection on, 154–155
sliding across continua of, 145–148,
146 (figure)
thinking and making meaning and,
141–144
Cognitive continua, 145–148, 146 (figure)
Cognitive demand, 9–10, 12, 137–140
Depth of Knowledge framework,
152–153
engagement qualities and, 63 (figure)
First Amendment Rights (freedoms) task
1, 28–30
First Amendment Rights (freedoms) task
2, 30–38
First Amendment Rights (freedoms) task
3, 38–44
First Amendment Rights (freedoms) task
4, 44–45, 46–49 (figure)
First Amendment Rights (freedoms) task
5, 50–53
reflection on tasks, 53–56
tasks at level 1 of, 20 (figure)
tasks at levels 3 and 4 of, 20, 21 (figure)
Cognitive engagement, 58–60,
60 (figure), 139
Cognitive expectation, 9–10
Common Core State Standards, 148
Connected learning, 37–38
engagement qualities and, 63 (figure)
First Amendment Rights (freedoms) task
1, 28–30
First Amendment Rights (freedoms) task
2, 30–38
First Amendment Rights (freedoms) task
3, 38–44
First Amendment Rights (freedoms) task
4, 44–45, 46–49 (figure)
First Amendment Rights (freedoms) task
5, 50–53
reflection on tasks, 53–56
Corso, M. J., 145
Council of Chief State School
Officers, 148
Creativity, 144–145
Curriculum
guaranteed access to, 161–162
trumping instruction, 160–161,
161 (figure)

Danielson, Charlotte, 57, 132
De Fockert, Jan, 153
DeJarnette, Chloe, 179
Depth of Knowledge framework,
152–153
Design components of tasks, 12–13

Diagnostic Instrument to Analyze
Learning (DIAL)
premises and research bases behind,
158–162, 159 (figure), 161 (figure)
three implementations of, 163–167,
164–165 (figure)
tips for using, 167–168
using the, 162–163, 164 (figure)
DIAL. See Diagnostic Instrument to
Analyze Learning (DIAL)
Digital tools. See Technology
Document Based Question (DBQ), 10
Doorbell Rang, The, 68
Dove, Rita, 125
Doyle, Walter, 8

Effective Schools, 161
Elmore, Richard, 7, 10
Encoding and memory, 153–154
Engagement
cognitive, 58–60, 60 (figure), 139
defining, 57–58
First Amendment Rights (freedoms) task
1, 28–30
First Amendment Rights (freedoms) task
2, 30–38
First Amendment Rights (freedoms) task
3, 38–44
First Amendment Rights (freedoms) task
4, 44–45, 46–49 (figure)
First Amendment Rights (freedoms) task
5, 50–53
interaction as, 64–67, 65 (figure), 68 (figure)
level versus thinking level, 88, 88 (figure)
versus participation, 58
qualities of, 11–13, 60–64, 61 (figure),
63 (figure), 68–71, 70 (figure)
reflection on tasks, 53–56
technology and, 72–73
volunteerism, 57
Engagement Cube, 13–15
Englehart, Max, 138
English, Fenwick, 160, 161
English Language Arts tasks, 171, 175,
180–184, 190–191
Enhancing Professional Practice: A
Framework for Teaching, 57
Evaluation and making meaning, 144
Ewing, Beth, 192

Faulkner, K., 135
Feraldi, Paulette, 165–166
Ferrington, Bruce, 92–93
First Amendment rights (freedoms) tasks
cognition continua and, 147–148
reflection on, 53–56

task 1 (list), 28–30
task 2 (picture), 30–38
task 3 (examples), 38–44
task 4 (event analysis), 44–45,
    46–49 (figure)
task 5 (consensus continuum), 50–53
Four Rs of Reflective Thinking, 90
Furst, Edward, 138

Garver, James R., 10, 139, 162
Gearlds, Tommy, 196
Generation and testing of hypotheses.
    See Hypotheses
Geography task, 193
Go Formative, 131
*Good Questions: Great Ways to
    Differentiate Mathematics
    Instruction,* 122
Google Classroom, 90, 130
Google Docs, 103
Google Forms, 131
Google Slides, 90, 91 (figure), 132
Graves, Stacy, 176
Green River Regional Educational
    Cooperative (GRREC), 13
Grossman, Lev, 91
Gunter, Angela, 191

Hail, Jennifer, 182
Hats Off for the Fourth of July, 146–147,
    146 (figure)
Hattie, John, 25, 124, 137
Hill, Walter, 138
Hunger Games, The, 78–79
Hutchins, Pat, 68
HyperDoc, 85–86, 86–87 (figure)
Hypotheses, 95–96
    feedback coming through extension
        of the task or presentation of
        additional stimulus, 97–106,
        98 (figure), 101–102 (figure),
        104–106 (figure)
    questions for generating and testing,
        129–130
    students having intellectual/emotional
        safety to find, articulate, explain, and
        stand by their, 96
    students having their findings validated
        to ensure they are logical,
        reasonable, and rational, 96–97

Iconic Event Task, 1–5
    rubric for analysis of, 21–23,
        22–23 (figure)
If the World Were a Village, 92–94,
    93 (figure)

Impressionist painting, 100–104,
    101–102 (figure), 104 (figure)
Instructional core, 7
Instructional Rounds in Education, 7
Interaction as engagement, 64–67,
    65 (figure), 68 (figure)
IPad, 67

Jackson, Robyn R., 195

Kahoot, 131
Keeler, Alice, 178
Krathwohl, David, 138–139

Landis, Sarah, 85–86
Leaders of Their Own Learning, 169
Learning through accepting meaning,
    140–141
Learning With Others, 37–38, 61–62
    See also Connected learning
Levi, L., 135
Lezotte, Larry, 161
Library media tasks, 172
Listening/watching activities, 11–12
Lovin, LouAnn, 136

Math cognition, 148–152
Mathematics tasks, 173–174, 176–179, 189
McDaniel, Kerrie, 188
Meaning
    analysis and, 142–144
    learning through accepted, 140–141
    making meaning on top of, 144–145
    thinking and making, 141–144
Medina, John, 64, 76
Memory and encoding, 153–154

Naming of thinking strategies, 98–100
National Council of Teachers of
    Mathematics (NCTM), 136–137, 148
National Governors' Association, 148
Never Underestimate Your Teachers, 195
No-fail writing tasks, 84 (figure)
Nonlinguistic representations, 91–95,
    93–95 (figure)
    questions, 129
Note-making, 97–98
    note-taking becoming, 83–89, 84 (figure),
        86–89 (figure)
    questions on, 128–129
    reflection in, 90, 91 (figure)
Note-taking
    becoming note-making, 83–89,
        84 (figure), 86–89 (figure)
    summarizing and, 79–83, 80 (figure),
        82 (figure)

"Old Answer to Humanity's Newest Problem: Data, The," 91–92
Open versus closed questions, 124–130
Ownbey, Rylee, 183, 195

Participation versus engagement, 58
Performance, tasks predicting, 10–12, 162
Pickering, Debra, 64
Poll Everywhere, 131
Powerful Task Rubric for Designing Student Work, 15–25, 169–170, 195–196
  academic strategies and, 76, 77 (figure)
  engagement qualities analysis, 63 (figure)
  English Language Arts tasks, 171, 175, 180–184, 190–191
  five rights (or freedoms) guaranteed in the First Amendment task 1 (list), 28–30
  five rights (or freedoms) guaranteed in the First Amendment task 2 (picture), 30–38
  five rights (or freedoms) guaranteed in the First Amendment task 3 (examples), 38–44
  five rights (or freedoms) guaranteed in the First Amendment task 4 (event analysis), 44–45, 46–49 (figure)
  geography task, 193
  at level 3 and 4 of cognitive demand, 21 (figure)
  at level 1 of cognitive demand, 20 (figure)
  library media tasks, 172
  math cognition and, 148–152
  mathematics tasks, 173–174, 176–179, 189
  nonlinguistic representations and, 91–95, 93–95 (figure)
  note-making (See Note-making)
  one content, five tasks example, 27–53
  original, 16–17 (figure)
  Personal Response reflection on, 53–56
  qualities of engagement and, 60–64, 61 (figure), 63 (figure)
  rubric for analysis of Iconic Events Task, 22–23 (figure)
  science task, 186–188
  social studies task, 185, 192–194
Pride and Prejudice, 104

Quaglia, Russell, 142, 145
Quality Questioning, 118
Questioning the answer questions, 125
Question(s)
  asking for a sentence of truth, 126
  changing the, 127

for generating and testing hypotheses, 129–130
  how to open, 124–130
  identifying similarities and differences, 127, 128 (figure)
  moving from closed to open, 123–124, 123 (figure)
  nonlinguistic representation, 129
  origin of, 109–111
  origins of teacher, 116–124, 118–119 (figure), 121 (figure), 123–124 (figure)
  questioning the answer, 125
  See-Think-Wonder, 111–116, 112–113 (figure)
  summarizing and note-making, 128–129
  technology and, 131–133
Quizziz, 131

Reeh, Trever, 189
Reflection
  on cognition, 154–155
  in note-making, 90, 91 (figure)
  on Powerful Task Rubric tasks, 53–56
Rigor in tasks, 31, 37–38, 69
  slippage, 152
Riley, Autumn, 175
Roosevelt, Franklin D., 96
Rugen, Leah, 169

Sattes, Beth, 118–119
School, definition of, 7
Science task, 186–188
See-Think-Wonder, 111–116, 112–113 (figure), 196
17,000 Classroom Visits Can't Be Wrong: Strategies That Engage Students, Promote Active Learning, and Boost Achievement, 13, 15
Sheffield, Jennifer, 187
Similarities and differences, identification of, 78–79, 127, 128 (figure)
Smith, David J., 92
Smith, Margaret Schwan, 148, 149 (figure), 152
Soapbox, 131
Social studies task, 185, 192–194
Socrative, 131
Stein, Mary Kay, 148, 149 (figure), 152
Stevens, Michael, 120
Stice, Terri, 13–15, 68–69, 196
  comparison of similarities, 65 (figure)
  educator awards, 159
Storey, Liz, 13
Student Voice, 142

Summarizing and note-taking, 79–83, 80 (figure), 82 (figure)
   questions, 128–129
Surface to deep learning, 137

Task(s)
   as activities, 10
   always including a cognitive expectation or demand, 9–10
   definition of, 7–8
   design components of, 12–13
   engagement and powered-up, 68–71, 70 (figure)
   English Language Arts, 171, 175, 180–184, 190–191
   geography, 193
   library media, 172
   mathematics, 173–174, 176–179, 189
   predicting performance, 10–12, 162
   relationship between activity and, 11–12
   rigor in, 31, 37–38, 69, 152
   science, 186–188
   social studies, 185, 192–194
   See also Powerful Task Rubric for Designing Student Work
Teaching Student-Centered Mathematics, 68
Technology, 29 (figure)
   and the Engagement Cube, 13–15
   nonlinguistic representations and, 91–92

questions and, 131–133
slicing in engaging qualities with, 72–73
TEDtalks, 87, 120–121
Thinking level, 88, 88 (figure)
Thinking strategies, 12
TIME Magazine, 91
Today's Meet, 131
Truth, sentences of, 126
2-5-8 choice menu, 185

Van De Walle, John, 136
Visible Learning for Mathematics, 137
Volunteerism, 57
Vsauce, 120–121

Walsh, Jake, 118–119
Webb, James, 152
Wilder, Sarah, 185
Woodfin, Libby, 169
Wordsworth, William, 142–144, 143 (figure)
Writing tasks, no-fail, 84 (figure)

York-Barr, Jennifer, 90
YouTube, 120

Ziefert, Harriet, 146–147, 146 (figure)

A SAGE Publishing Company

CORWIN HAS ONE MISSION: to enhance education through intentional professional learning.

We build long-term relationships with our authors, educators, clients, and associations who partner with us to develop and continuously improve the best evidence-based practices that establish and support lifelong learning.

Solutions you want. Experts you trust. Results you need.